Behaviour Change for Sustainability

Adam Corner
The Climate Outreach and Information Network (COIN)

Gareth Kane
Terra Infirma Ltd

Paula Owen
Paula Owen Consulting & Eco Action Games

First published in 2014 by Dō Sustainability
87 Lonsdale Road, Oxford OX2 7ET, UK

ISBN 978-1-909293-95-3 (eBook-ePub)
ISBN 978-1-909293-96-0 (eBook-PDF)
ISBN 978-1-909293-94-6 (Paperback)

A catalogue record for this title is available from the British Library.

Dō Sustainability strives for net positive social and environmental impact. See our sustainability policy at **www.dosustainability.com**.

Page design and typesetting by Alison Rayner
Cover by Becky Chilcott

For further information on Dō Sustainability, visit our website: **www.dosustainability.com**

DōShorts

Dō Sustainability is the publisher of DōShorts: short, high-value ebooks that distil sustainability best practice and business insights for busy, results-driven professionals. Each DōShort can be read in 90 minutes.

New and forthcoming DōShorts -- stay up to date

We publish new DōShorts each month. The best way to keep up to date? Sign up to our short, monthly newsletter. Go to **www.dosustainability.com/newsletter** to sign up to the Dō Newsletter. Some of our latest and forthcoming titles include:

- *Understanding G4: The Concise Guide to Next Generation Sustainability Reporting* Elaine Cohen
- *Leading Sustainable Innovation* Nick Coad & Paul Pritchard
- *Leadership for Sustainability and Change* Cynthia Scott & Tammy Esteves
- *The Social Licence to Operate: Your Management Framework for Complex Times* Leeora Black
- *Building a Sustainable Supply Chain* Gareth Kane
- *Management Systems for Sustainability: How to Successfully Connect Strategy and Action* Phil Cumming
- *Understanding Integrated Reporting: The Concise Guide to Integrated Thinking and the Future of Corporate Reporting* Carol Adams
- *Networks for Sustainability: Harnessing People Power to Deliver Your Goals* Sarah Holloway
- *Making Sustainability Matter: How to Make Materiality Drive Profit, Strategy and Communications* Dwayne Baraka

DōShorts Toolbox

Suitable for personal and organisational libraries, each Toolbox collects 3-4 thematically related DōShorts, forming an indispensable compendium of strategies and techniques on a broader sustainability challenge. New and forthcoming titles include:

- *Behaviour Change for Sustainability*
- *Better Corporate Reporting*
- *Sustainability for SMEs*

Subscriptions

In addition to individual sales of our ebooks, we now offer subscriptions. Access 60+ ebooks for the price of 6 with a personal subscription to our full e-library. Institutional subscriptions are also available for your staff or students. Visit **www.dosustainability.com/books/subscriptions** or email **veruschka@dosustainability.com**

Write for us, or suggest a DōShort

Please visit **www.dosustainability.com** for our full publishing programme. If you don't find what you need, write for us! Or Suggest a DōShort on our website. We look forward to hearing from you.

Contents

**Promoting Sustainable Behaviour:
A practical guide to what works**

How much of a difference can changes in individual behaviour make? Isn't climate change – and the challenge of sustainability more generally – just too big a problem for individuals and communities to worry about? Why focus on the behaviour of ordinary people when political agreements and technological advances will do more to tackle climate change than anything an individual could achieve?

The way that a message about sustainable behaviour is 'framed' (the language used, the associations that are triggered, and the reasons that are given for it) will have a big impact on how people respond to it. And different ways of framing a message speak to very different values. Understanding how to structure messages about sustainable behaviour so that they have the biggest impact in the long term is the aim of this chapter.

3   Harnessing The Power Of Social Norms......25

We are social creatures, and we take a lot of our cues about how to behave from those around us. Many strategies for promoting sustainable behaviour seem to forget this, and focus exclusively on people as individuals. But by paying attention to social norms (the standards that we use to judge the appropriateness of our own behaviour), a much stronger sense of collective momentum can be generated, making any programme to promote sustainable behaviour much more likely to succeed.

4 Breaking Bad Habits and Creating Good Ones

Habits – good and bad – define us, and un-sustainable behaviour is often a product of un-conscious thought-processes. Getting to grips with how to break bad habits, and create good ones, is the focus of this chapter.

5 Using Scare Tactics: Does It Work?

Climate change – and the challenge of getting to grips with sustainability – can seem daunting. A lot of attempts at promoting sustainable behaviour fail because they simply make people feel guilty and don't inspire action. So what is the best way of warning people about the serious risks of climate change, without making them switch off?

6 Putting It All Together: Making Wider Change 47

How does promoting sustainable behaviour fit into the bigger picture? This chapter highlights the importance of social networks, catalysing reciprocal change from employers and at a political level, and sustaining change over time.

Appendix A: Mapping Principles to Case Studies

Appendix A maps the principles for promoting sustainable behaviour and the case studies of good and bad practice described in the book in one easy-to-use table.

Appendix B: Promoting Sustainable Behaviour – The People and Projects That You Need to Know About

Appendix B highlights the people and projects that are essential resources for promoting sustainable behaviour.

Green Jujitsu: The Smart Way to Embed Sustainability into Your Organisation

CONTENTS

How Gamification Can Help Your Business Engage in Sustainability

An innovative, novel engagement theory has permeated the business world over recent years. In a relatively short time the ideas behind 'gamification' have begun to circulate through the corporate community and beyond, and are now causing widening ripples of interest in diverse sectors of society. This DōShort investigates the thinking around gamification in this early stage of its evolution and asks the question: how may it play a part in advancing the sustainability engagement agenda?

This section discusses what gamification is. It is currently touted by global players and thought-leaders as the new business tech trend to watch, and is already being tested out in a diverse range of sectors, but what does the term actually mean and what do its theories entail in practice? Crucially, could it have relevance to the sustainability sector?

The case to prove whether gamification will be a useful long-term engagement tool for sustainability is still in its infancy. To date it has shown early promise and delivered some impressive results in other sectors, medical research and health and fitness applications being stand out examples. Its use as a sustainability engagement tool has also delivered some initial early success stories in areas of transport, employee engagement, energy and recycling as described in this book. In this section we explore the potential for future gamification in sustainability and make suggestions for how a business could develop its own sustainability 'game plan'.

Promoting Sustainable Behaviour

A practical guide to what works

Adam Corner

Head of Talking Climate Programme,
The Climate Outreach and Information Network (COIN),
Old Music Hall, 106–108 Cowley Road,
Oxford OX4 1JE, United Kingdom.
Email: adam@coinet.org.uk
Web: www.coinet.org.uk

Climate Outreach and
Information Network

Climate Outreach and Information Network is a charity established in 2004, dedicated to helping people communicate climate change more effectively.

Abstract

PROMOTING SUSTAINABLE BEHAVIOUR is a critical part of society's response to climate change. The aim of this short and practically focused book is to show how to make the most of campaigns to promote sustainable behaviour – in households, when commuting, in the workplace and beyond. There are more and less effective ways of encouraging people to act in a more sustainable way, and some important pitfalls to avoid. But by summarising 'what works' and pulling out the most important take-home messages, this book contains the tools for maximising the success of any sustainable behaviour initiative. By looking beyond individual behaviours and thinking more about people's identities and values; by considering the social signals that provide such important cues for our everyday behaviour; by using the best strategies to attract (and keep) people's interest; and by understanding how to break bad habits and create good ones, this guide to promoting sustainable behaviour offers the best chance of making a sustainable behaviour campaign work.

About The Author

DR ADAM CORNER is a researcher and writer whose work focuses on the psychology of communicating climate change. He leads the Talking Climate programme for the Climate Outreach and Information Network (a charity which specialises in climate change communication), and is a Research Associate in the School of Psychology at Cardiff University, UK. He has published widely in leading academic journals, writes regularly for the *Guardian* newspaper and other national media, and edits the website 'Talking Climate' (**www.talkingclimate.org**), the gateway to research on climate change communication.

Adam's work aims to bridge the gap between academic research and the range of groups – policy-makers, practitioners, businesses and community groups – who can make best use of it.

CHAPTER 1

Promoting Sustainable Behaviour: What's The Point?

HOW MUCH OF A DIFFERENCE can changes in individual behaviour make? Isn't climate change – and the challenge of sustainability more generally – just too big a problem for individuals and communities to worry about? Why focus on the behaviour of ordinary people when political agreements and technological advances will do more to tackle climate change than anything an individual could achieve?

These are all critical questions for anyone interested in promoting sustainable behaviour – whether at home or in the workplace – to ask themselves. After all, if it were possible to wave a magic low-carbon wand and solve climate change overnight through new technologies, the strict regulation of high-polluting industries, or a binding political agreement that all the world's countries signed up to, wouldn't that make more sense than focusing on everyday attitudes and behaviour?

The problem, of course, is that there is no magic low-carbon wand – but even if there were, it would be waved by a person as susceptible to the quirks, biases and pitfalls of human judgement as anyone else. While it is comforting to draw sharp distinctions between politics, technology and individuals, the reality is that human behaviour underpins it all. Political parties will not pass legislation that is patently unpopular among the electorate. Technological advances can provide low-carbon alternatives like electric buses, but a zero-emissions bus will have zero passengers unless people decide to use it. And even the most carefully planned policy interventions can backfire if they don't take account of how people – the wildcard in any equation – will respond.

For example, if a driver who replaces their car with a fuel-efficient model takes advantage of the cheaper running costs and drives further and more often, then the amount of carbon saved is clearly reduced. This is what's known as a 'rebound' effect – one of many pitfalls that plague well-intentioned campaigns to promote sustainable behaviour. Rebound effects like these – where people take two steps forward and one step back – occur because no single behaviour takes place in a vacuum.

Consider campaigns in other areas of life. If the end-result of a television advert to promote the use of seatbelts was that drivers felt safer and drove faster, the ad would only be considered a partial success. If a drive to end teenage obesity resulted in an increase in the number of adolescents with self-image problems and eating disorders, this undermines the value of the campaign. And sustainable behaviours are no different – they have to be seen as small parts of a bigger picture, not isolated and separated from their wider impacts.

Studies have found[1] that on average, only about two-thirds of the calculated carbon reductions for a given household action (e.g. lowering the thermostat or reducing food waste) are likely to be achieved in reality. This is because money saved on the heating bill is (potentially) money available for a flight abroad, or some other high-carbon activity.

Promoting sustainable behaviour is not necessarily as easy as it first appears, but this is where simple, easy-to-apply and practical advice about 'what works' comes in. The aim of this short and practically focused book is to show how to make the most of campaigns to promote sustainable behaviour – in households, when commuting, in the workplace and beyond.

Simple and painless?

Generating long-lasting and meaningful changes in sustainable behaviour is a huge challenge. When first confronted with this issue, many people assumed that the problem was simply a lack of information – that once people knew how environmentally damaging their actions were, they'd soon start making changes. Unfortunately, the 'pamphlet approach' to sustainable behaviour has only had limited effectiveness – public information campaigns need more than just a clever slogan and the right information in order to succeed.[2]

Many sustainability initiatives over the past half a decade have responded to this by targeting low-hanging fruit – so-called 'simple and painless' behaviour changes like unplugging phone chargers, switching to energy-saving light-bulbs, or re-using plastic bags. The idea – which makes intuitive sense – is that these simple changes provide a 'way in', and may act as a catalyst for more substantial changes (in terms of energy saved) in the future.

Unfortunately, there is only limited evidence that starting with simple and painless changes is necessarily the best way of catalysing further changes – and there is a risk that people will feel they have 'done their bit'.[3] As Box 1 shows, there is a huge difference in the carbon-saving impact of different behaviours, but seldom is this reflected in sustainable behaviour initiatives.

These examples illustrate an important point: that it is possible to 'do behaviour change' in better or worse ways. Focusing on activities that have only a tiny payoff in terms of energy use can only be justified if they are the first step on a ladder that leads to more significant energy savings, something that the evidence presented in this book can help with. If low-impact changes (including things like switching off a few lights around the office) become an end in themselves, then the effort expended is probably not worth it. But if a strategy for promoting sustainable behaviour is as evidence-based as possible, engages with people at a deeper level than single behaviours, and gives thought to how people's personal values and social identities shape a wide range of behaviours, then there are important – in fact, essential – gains to be made in terms of building a sustainable society.

Behaviour change matters

In both the private and public sectors, it is now widely accepted that reducing energy consumption is a key battleground for tackling carbon emissions. The UK government – although falling well short of its claim to be the 'greenest ever' – is pushing ahead with ambitious plans that should (if they are successful) see significant changes in energy use among householders. 'Smart' energy meters are gradually being rolled out, and the flagship 'Green Deal' aims to insulate millions of homes by 2020.

Installing wall or cavity insulation might seem like a good example of a change in people's living arrangements that is purely technical – something that doesn't require thinking about people's attitudes or behaviours. But as the sustainable behaviour specialists Alexa Spence and Nick Pidgeon from Cardiff University have argued,[4] changes in household insulation depend on some key assumptions. In particular, the overheating of residential buildings has to become socially unacceptable, and people will have to be motivated to make changes to their home heating routines if they are not to fall into the 'rebound' trap. These are behavioural issues, not technical ones.

So promoting sustainable behaviour matters and ensuring that any sustainable programme is based on the best available research and practical case studies is an essential piece of the puzzle. Many people are wary of committing themselves to changes in their personal behaviour when it seems as if bigger gains can be made elsewhere. But unless people can identify with and understand climate change and sustainability at a personal level, those political and technological shifts will simply never happen. It is not a choice between technologies, policies and changing behaviour – the transition to a sustainable, low-carbon society requires all three.

So this book is for anyone who wants to ensure that their sustainable behaviour campaign – in the workplace or beyond – stands the best chance of working, and doesn't fall victim to the traps into which too many well-intentioned sustainability initiatives fall.

Each of the following chapters focuses on a different aspect of promoting sustainable behaviour, and is designed with practical outcomes in mind. The structure of each chapter includes a quick-start, 'what you need to know' summary at the outset, plus a case study, essential background theory that holds it all together, and advice on how to put this theory into practice.

....

BOX 1: Sustainable behaviours – making the most impact
Something so often missing from conversations about sustainable behaviour is how different actions stack up against each other. Does it matter if everyone leaves their phone-chargers plugged in? Is it better to car-share or ride to work on a half-empty bus? And how many years would you have to buy low-carbon orange juice for before you saved the same amount of carbon as avoiding one return flight between Spain and the UK?*

This box sets out some well-known sustainable behaviours – colour-coded to show how much energy they are likely to save. Keeping information like this close at hand helps to make an intimidatingly complex problem more manageable: don't spend too much time worrying about phone-chargers if there's a chance of targeting something more significant.

It's important to keep a sense of proportion by focusing on the big wins. In an office, space heating and air conditioning are better targets than lighting and standby settings. It's also worth asking yourself whether you would like to be bugged about certain things – no-one really wants to be told how to make a cup of tea, and so although boiling the kettle more efficiently will save energy, it might also make enemies of the very people you want to reach. An eco-kettle that does the job for people might be more sensible in this case.

It's also worth busting some popular myths about energy-saving. In buildings, air conditioning is often the largest consumer of electricity. In an office, computers, printers and faxes will probably use far more electricity than lighting. Low energy bulbs do take half a minute to fully warm up, but they use no more energy during this time than they do when they are on. Although lighting is not the biggest drain on energy, it is worth turning them off – even for a short time – and it won't shorten their life either. About 2 kg of carbon is saved for every short journey that is made using a bike or on foot instead of a car. Switching to an energy-efficient light-bulb only saves 10 kg over a whole year – so getting to grips with your commuting can have a significant impact.

But if swapping a car journey for a bike ride is a good idea, then swapping a flight for a train journey is even better. London to Paris by Eurostar uses about 90% less carbon than taking a flight – and flying is by far and away the most energy-intensive way of travelling (unless you are partial to pan-European road trips in monster 4x4 trucks with no companions with whom to split your carbon footprint).

HIGH IMPACT

Avoiding a flight – or cutting it out altogether. A plane is almost always the most carbon-intensive way of travelling. European trains – unlike British ones – are mostly fast and reliable.

Cycling to work – an average car sitting in a traffic jam in rush hour wastes 100 kg of carbon over a week. Cycling is essentially carbon-free.

Insulating a loft/roof space – over 40 years an impressive 35 tonnes of carbon can be saved (about three years worth of the average British carbon footprint)

MEDIUM IMPACT

Computing equipment – older, slower, desktop machines use more power than energy-efficient laptops (which also tend to switch themselves off). But the biggest impact of computing equipment is in the production of it, not the electricity to run it. So buying new kit for the sake of it is not necessarily a good idea.

Lighting – low energy light-bulbs use around a fifth of the electricity old-fashioned ones. The more you replace, the more you save.

Laundry – washing clothes at lower temperatures (30 degrees) and drying them naturally uses about a sixth of the energy compared to high-temperature washes plus tumble drying. Over a year this adds up.

LOW IMPACT

Plastic bags – although there are good reasons to avoid unnecessary waste, the carbon impact of a plastic bag is minimal.

Mobile phone-chargers – there is no reason not to unplug them when not in use, and newer phones need charging more often and absorb a lot more power. But phone-chargers plugged in pale in comparison to TVs and other electrical equipment on standby.

SOURCES: 5,6

* Researchers from the Tyndall Centre calculated that you would have to make 32 years' worth of daily purchases of 'lower carbon' Tesco orange juice to save the same amount of carbon as avoiding just one return flight from the UK to Spain.

Box 1 is intended to give you a flavour of the relative impact of different actions that people can take around the home or on the move. But for more detailed information on the carbon savings of specific changes, use the Energy Saving Trust website, and the interactive tools and resources it contains: **http://www.energysavingtrust.org.uk/**.

....

CHAPTER 2

Framing Your Messages: What Values Are You Appealing To?

What you need to know

THE WAY THAT A MESSAGE about sustainable behaviour is 'framed' (the language used, the associations that are triggered, and the reasons that are given for it) will have a big impact on how people respond to it. And different ways of framing a message speak to very different values. Understanding how to structure messages about sustainable behaviour so that they have the biggest impact in the long term is the aim of this chapter.

A value is usually defined as a 'guiding principle in the life of a person'. Over several decades, and through research conducted in over 60 countries,[7] there is now a huge body of evidence that shows that certain values and beliefs tend to go together, while others tend to be opposed to each other. There are two broad categories of values, which are known as 'self-enhancing' and 'self-transcending'. People who identify strongly with 'self-enhancing' or 'extrinsic' values (e.g. materialism, personal ambition) tend not to identify strongly with 'self-transcending' or 'intrinsic' values (e.g. benevolence, respect for the environment).

FRAMING YOUR MESSAGES:
WHAT VALUES ARE YOU APPEALING TO?

There are some important practical implications to this research: people who hold 'self-transcendent' values (especially pro-environmental values and high levels of altruism) are more likely to engage in sustainable behaviour,[8] show higher concern about environmental risks like climate change,[9] are more likely to engage in specific sustainable behaviours such as recycling[10] and are more likely to support policies to tackle climate change.[11]

> *This means that unless campaigns to promote sustainable behaviour make an attempt to target 'self-transcending' values, they may inadvertently promote precisely the types of personal and cultural values that will make sustainable behaviour less likely in the longer term. And this is why the way that messages and campaigns are 'framed' is so important.*

Consider two different ways of encouraging people to car-share on the commute to work. One option would be to tell people how much money they will save on petrol. This would be a 'self-enhancing' reason for car-sharing – and there is no doubt that appealing to people's wallets may be an effective way of selling the idea of car-sharing to them. A second option would be to emphasise the environmental benefits of car-sharing. This would be a 'self-transcendent' reason for car-sharing because it does not (directly) benefit individuals. This may also be an effective way of encouraging people to car-share.

If the challenge of sustainability was simply to sign as many people up to car-sharing schemes as possible, then the choice would be simple: go with the one that is most effective. But of course, the challenge of sustainability is vastly more complex than this, which means that anyone seeking to promote sustainable behaviour has to ask 'what happens next?'

> *Research suggests that in order to create a situation where one behavioural change will lead to another, it is important to focus on self-transcending values and environmental reasons for sustainable behaviour.*

The key to promoting meaningful changes in sustainable behaviour – that do more than just pay lip service to tackling climate change – is to nurture and develop a sense of environmental identity or citizenship.[12,13] When a person acts for self-interested reasons, that person will perceive themselves as someone who does things for their own benefit. They will only engage in further sustainable behaviours if there is something in it for them – as soon as the 'sweeteners' dry up, so will their interest in sustainability.

But if people begin to think of themselves as 'someone who does things for the environment', the chance that they will engage in other sustainable behaviours is much higher. It may not always be the quickest way of promoting a specific sustainable behaviour, but ultimately people can figure out for themselves whether something is in their own interest or not. The job of a sustainable behaviour practitioner is to help them see the bigger picture, and make the arguments about sustainability that an appeal to their wallet cannot do.

If you only do one thing...

Think really carefully about how to ensure that promoting sustainable behaviour works in the long, as well as the short term. Make a list of all the possible reasons you can think of for engaging in a particular behaviour that you're interested in (e.g. encouraging car-sharing). Divide them into 'self-interested' and 'self-transcendent' groups, and before you reach for the money-saving lever, try to construct a *less self-serving way of framing your message.*

The theory that makes it work

One of the defining debates within the environmental movement over the past decade has been between those who believe that applying the techniques and strategies of marketing physical products is the best way of promoting sustainable behaviour (social marketing), and those who have argued that this approach – trying to 'sell' climate change – is ultimately counterproductive unless the right underlying values are targeted by campaigns, and unless the messages are 'framed' in a way that encourages sustainable behaviours across the board.

In some ways, this debate is less about the best way of achieving immediate changes in sustainable behaviour than it is about the best way of achieving sustained and consistent changes over a longer period of time. A recent study by researchers at Cardiff University[14] found that framing a sustainable behaviour – car-sharing – in two different ways had an impact on how likely people were to engage in other sustainable behaviours. In an experiment, some people were primed to think about the environmental benefits of car-sharing, while others were encouraged to think about financial reasons for this activity. The people who had considered environmental reasons for car-sharing were more likely to subsequently recycle, showing that the reasons given for one sustainable behaviour impact on the chance that people will engage in other sustainable behaviours in the future.

Intentionally or unintentionally, all information is 'framed' by the context in which it appears. This could mean the individual words and phrases that are used (sometimes called 'conceptual framing'), and is more akin to the 'spin' that is put on a message (like describing a product as containing 50% less fat, when in fact it still contains more fat than any of its competitors).

But framing can also mean something more substantial, and this is called 'deep framing'. 'Deep framing' refers to the connections that are forged between a particular communication strategy or public policy and a set of deeper values or principles,[15] and offers one method of linking climate change engagement strategies with self-transcendent values.[16] For example, putting a financial value on an endangered species, and building an economic case for their conservation, makes them equivalent (at the level of deep frames) to other 'assets' of the same value (like a hotel chain). This is a very different frame to one that attempts to achieve the same conservation goals through emphasising the intrinsic value of rare animal species, as something that should be protected in their own right.

Looking beyond sustainable behaviour, the animal rights charity PETA is notorious for its adverts which promote vegetarianism (but do so through images of scantily clad women). Critics say that they are doing more harm than good, by promoting misogynistic values. So it is clear that a message can cause 'collateral damage', even if it doesn't intend to.

Putting the theory into practice

Everyone has both self-enhancing and self-transcending values (we have all, at some point, treasured a material possession – but we have also all valued the health of a family member). People who promote sustainability do not (and should not) seek to try and 'change' people's values. But instead of stoking up self-interest, campaigns for sustainable behaviour can instead nurture and strengthen self-transcending values.

Certainly, this means 'meeting people where they are' as much as possible. Depending on your audience, different messages and ways of approaching the problem are appropriate. But there are limits on how far the meaning of a message about sustainable behaviour can be bent before it becomes broken and meaningless. Some things (regular flying or eating imported red meat everyday) are simply unsustainable, and pretending otherwise is in no-one's best interest.

The trick is to develop and apply 'bridges' between what you want to say (the message about sustainability) and the issues that your audience are interested in, but without inadvertently promoting values that make sustainable behaviours less achievable in the longer term.

The bridges that can link your message and your audience are probably best identified by exploring the issue you want to address with a few people, and getting a sense of what might motivate them to change their behaviour.

Case study

A recent report called 'Common Cause', written for charitable organisations who frequently design campaigns to reach large numbers of people, applies the 'values and frames' thinking to a number of practical issues. The central argument of the Common Cause report is that for 'bigger-than-self' problems like climate change (i.e. problems that may not be in an individual's immediate self-interest to invest energy and resources in helping to solve), campaigns that propagate or endorse self-enhancing values may actually undermine the 'common cause' that links them.

Although this report was aimed at charities, its lessons can equally be applied to strategies for promoting sustainable behaviour. There is no point in undermining the argument that tackling climate change through sustainable behaviour is a shared challenge by focusing on the ways that sustainable behaviour may serve people's self-interest. This is undoubtedly an effective way of getting a single, well-defined behavioural change achieved – but at what cost?

Find out more

www.valuesandframes.org: the go-to resource for the latest thinking on using the right values and frames for sustainability.

http://www.wastewatch.org.uk/: an organisation which has been carefully applying these kinds of insights to their work with good practical examples.

....

·

CHAPTER 3

Harnessing The Power
Of Social Norms

What you need to know

IT IS VERY RARE THAT PEOPLE ACT purely as individuals. We are social creatures, and we take a lot of our cues about how to behave from those around us, whether this is family, friends, colleagues or even strangers on the commute to work. Many strategies for promoting sustainable behaviour seem to forget this and focus exclusively on people as individuals.

This means that they are working against the grain of human nature and making the challenge of sustainability feel more overwhelming than it actually is. But by paying attention to social norms (the standards that we use to judge the appropriateness of our own behaviour), a much stronger sense of collective momentum can be generated, making any programme to promote sustainable behaviour much more likely to succeed.

The basic idea is that people tend to act in a way that is socially acceptable, and so if a particular behaviour (littering, for example, or driving a car with a large engine) can be cast in a socially unacceptable light, then people should be less likely to engage in it.

HARNESSING THE POWER
OF SOCIAL NORMS

> *No-one likes to feel like they are acting in a way that their friends or colleagues don't approve of. So communicating the idea that sustainable behaviour is 'the norm' is a powerful tool.*

Pictures and videos of ordinary people ('like me') engaging in sustainable behaviours are a simple and effective way of generating a sense of social normality around saving energy.[17] Encouraging people to make public commitments (for example, signing up to make a specific change to their behaviour on a shared notice board) is another simple way of making 'private' behaviours 'public'. And studies have shown that when hotel guests are provided with information that other guests are re-using their towels, they are more likely to do this as well, over and above the impact of telling them about the environmental benefits.[18]

> *However, there is a danger that strategies based on social norms can backfire if they accidentally communicate the fact that lots of people are engaging in unsustainable behaviour.*

For example, a campaign focusing on the fact that too many people take internal flights actually contains two messages: that taking internal flights is bad for the environment and that lots of people are taking internal flights. This second message can make the campaign counterproductive: by conveying how common internal flights are, it can give those who do not currently take short-haul flights a perverse incentive to do so.

So use social norms carefully, and consider what information people will take from them. It is crucial to focus not only on what people are doing, but also on what they should be doing.

If you only do one thing...

Everyone has a peer group and a social network. Before you begin any campaign to promote sustainable behaviour, ask yourself who this group is for the people you are targeting, and try to ensure that your initiative has a social visibility, and is not simply restricted to personal emails or leaflets in people's pigeon holes. More than any information or facts you can give them, your audience will take their cues as to whether sustainable behaviour is something weird or something normal from their social group.

The theory that makes it work

Social norms are a powerful and effective way of influencing sustainable behaviours, but there are some pitfalls to avoid. As Robert Cialdini and his colleagues at Arizona State University have demonstrated repeatedly, the problem with appeals based on social norms is that they often contain a hidden message.[18] So, for example, in an experiment led by the psychologist Wesley Schultz,[17] researchers examined the influence of social norms on the household energy consumption of residents of California. The researchers picked houses at random and then divided them into groups depending on whether their energy consumption was higher or lower than the average for that area. Some low energy-use households received only information about average energy usage, thereby setting the social norm. A second group of low-energy households had a positive 'emoticon' (happy face) positioned next to their personal energy figure, conveying approval of their energy footprint. A third group of over-consuming households were shown their energy usage coupled with a negative emoticon (sad face), intended to convey disapproval of their higher-than-average footprint.

The researchers then measured energy consumption in the following months. As one might expect, the over-consuming households used the social norm as a motivation to reduce their energy use, but the under-consuming households that had received only the social norm information increased their energy use. Crucially though, the under-consuming households that had received positive feedback did not show this boomerang effect: the addition of a 'smiley face' next to their energy usage made all the difference. Despite the simplicity of the feedback, households that felt their under-consumption was socially approved (rather than a reason to relax) and maintained their small energy footprint. This suggests that using social norms can be effective, but only if they are used in the right way.

There are other ways of using social norms that don't rely on pointing to a 'silent majority' who are already engaging in a particular behaviour (because for many sustainable behaviours, positive norms are simply not there to promote). The Wasting Water is Weird (**http://wastingwaterisweird.com**) campaign uses a series of short videos to position wasting water as something only 'weird' people do. In the videos, a creepy, menacing character called Rip enthuses about wasting water, while someone 'ordinary' wastes water by, for example, leaving the tap on while brushing their teeth. The obvious implication is that if you waste water you are as socially undesirable as Rip.

In this campaign, social norms are being deployed to make a 'bad' behaviour appear to be the choice of a minority, neatly getting around the problem of no obvious 'good' social norms being readily available. But there is a risk with this type of approach, too: if the majority of people viewing the advert identify with the ordinary character, they may feel castigated and demonised for something that everyone else seems to view as normal.

Putting the theory into practice

Social norms are a fantastic method of amplifying the influence of existing good behaviours, but they can't bring about these good behaviours on their own. This means that social norm approaches have to be combined with more direct strategies for promoting sustainable behaviour in order to be effective, such as breaking habits down into manageable chunks (Chapter 4), or developing a sense of environmental responsibility that goes beyond individual behaviours (Chapter 2).

> *First, the right norms need to be created, then the power of social norm strategies can be fully realised.*

There are different reasons that people adopt social norms, and encouraging people to adopt a sustainable behaviour simply to 'conform', to avoid a feeling of guilt, or for fear of not 'fitting in', can lead to problems. Unfortunately, as the growing amount of 'greenwash' shows, the idea of sustainability can be a remarkably effective way of shifting patently unsustainable products.

We may currently compete through demonstrations of conspicuous material consumption, but material goods are simply a marker for social status. It's the social status that's important, and the markers we use to signify it can easily change.

> *We have a natural desire to try to out-do each other, and we will compete on whatever criteria happen to be around. But if people are only going green 'to be seen', then their level of engagement with the broader issue of sustainability is likely to be fairly shallow.*

If the use of social norms can be combined with an appeal to people's 'intrinsic' motivations (e.g. a sense of social belonging – see Chapter 2), they are likely to be more effective and persistent.

Case study

Academic research on social norms is now being put into practice by the energy company Opower, who have achieved small but consistent savings on average energy use with their US customers.[19] Opower's approach is deceptively simple: every customer who receives an energy bill also receives information about how much energy they are using relative to their neighbours. The energy bills that Opower customers receive show average usage relative to immediate neighbours ('people like them'), give feedback about recent bills (through positive or negative emoticons) and contain tips for saving energy.

Opower is are now trialling similar techniques in the UK. The hope is that when combined with improvements to household insulation made possible through the government's 'green deal', and 'smart' energy meters that can monitor not only household-level use, but room-by-room and appliance-by-appliance, significant reductions in energy use will be achieved.

Find out more

Find out more about Opower's use of social norms
for reducing energy bills
(http://opower.com/what-is-opower/reports/)

CHAPTER 4

Breaking Bad Habits and Creating Good Ones

What you need to know

HOW DOES YOUR AVERAGE DAY START? More than likely with a bleary-eyed stampede to get out of the house and into work, most of which is done on auto-pilot. For a species that prides itself on its unique consciousness, we do an awful lot of things without much conscious awareness.

> *Habits – good and bad – define us, and un-sustainable behaviour is often a product of un-conscious thought processes.*

A huge amount of household energy use is embedded in habitual behaviours. This is one of the reasons that despite good intentions we often fail to make changes that would reduce the amount of energy we use. We know that we *could* get the bus to work, but something always gets in the way (no umbrella for the walk to the bus stop or an out-of-date timetable). We know that re-using shopping bags is a small and simple way to reduce waste, but somehow, we only remember this once we arrive at the shop. We are not used to thinking through the energy-use implications of our behaviours, but we can if we need to, and there is a reliable body of research that shows how.

BREAKING BAD HABITS AND
CREATING GOOD ONES

> *The problem is that something seemingly straightforward like getting the bus to work is actually made up of lots of smaller (habitual) decisions, all of which can derail even the best intentions.*

One strategy for dealing with this challenge that has been developed over a number of years by studying how habits form (and how they change), involves breaking habitual behaviours down into 'if...then' style plans.

Driving to work might not seem like a 'habit', but break down what needs to happen to change this behaviour and it soon becomes clear that there is a lot of non-conscious decision-making going on beneath the surface. Most of the barriers to changing a behaviour can only be addressed by getting down to a level of detail that doesn't come naturally to most of us. And even though some of the steps might seem trivial, it is exactly these sorts of minor details that can wreck the best-laid plans.

Research has shown that forming even very strong *overall* goal intentions (without breaking the behaviour down into smaller chunks) leaves a large gap between intention and action. In particular, people can fail to get started (because there is no specified starting point) and can get derailed along the way (because there are not enough markers of progress).

Periods of *transition*, where routines are already in flux, provide useful opportunities to develop new, more sustainable habits. In the context of home insulation, some building work already scheduled for the house might provide not only the practical opportunity for some low-carbon upgrades, but also the perfect chance for making some long-intended changes to habits and routines.

Campaigns and initiatives based on these strategies have a proven track for behaviours as diverse as driving, recycling and increasing purchases of organic food.

> *The bottom line is that breaking behaviours down into small parts helps to bridge the infamous gap between good intentions and achieving outcomes, making planned changes in behaviour more likely to be realised.*

If you only do one thing...

Pick a high-impact sustainable behaviour from Box 1 in Chapter 1 that you think it is possible to have an impact on, and break it down into its most basic components. For each component, make an 'if...then' plan to ensure that achieving your overall goal is not obstructed by a hidden, habitual component of the behaviour.

The theory that makes it work

The basic idea behind changing bad habits and creating good ones is that any habitual behaviour can be broken down into sets of *intended* actions that are *implemented* as part of an overall goal. Breaking habits down into distinct *'implementation intentions'* allows not only the constituent parts of a certain behaviour to be identified, but also the barriers that might prevent *changing* that behaviour.[20]

To form an implementation intention, a person must first identify a response that is important for goal attainment and, second, anticipate a critical cue to initiate that response. For example, a person might specify a behaviour ('choose healthy option from menu'), and a situational cue with which to trigger it ('when I am reading the menu outside of the restaurant'). Making a detailed plan like this, which is contingent on situational cues, allows changes to be made if necessary – in this case, because the menu has been checked for healthy options before entering the restaurant, the diner can choose to move on if there are no healthy options on the menu (rather than be forced to choose an unhealthy option once seated). However, while they allow flexibility, they also tap into 'good' habits and the person does not need to think or deliberate too much about what to do next: there are specific 'if-then' rules to guide the way.

Implementation intentions have been used to successfully influence behaviour relating to driving behaviour,[21] consumer habits,[22] workplace recycling[23] and increasing the amount that people use public transport and buy organic food.[24] The strategy used in the study to encourage people to use buses more frequently was very simple: some people were asked to make a specific plan including a day and time for taking a new bus route to their university, whereas others were just asked to commit to using the bus more (at some point). Adding a financial incentive did not have any additional impact over and above making a step-by-step plan.

Putting the theory into practice

A central theme of this book is that although sustainable behaviour in general is important, focusing too much on *single* behaviours – particularly if they have only a limited impact in terms of energy saved – can be problematic. However, sometimes it makes sense to pick a behaviour (or related set of behaviours) to focus on, and these examples give an idea of the habitual components hiding within seemingly straightforward behaviours.

BOX 2

Example A: Getting the bus to work, instead of driving

Overall goal: Get the bus to work on Thursdays and Fridays

Breaking down the goal:

IF... it is Wednesday or Thursday evening, *THEN* set the alarm clock early enough to allow extra time to get to work.

IF it is Wednesday or Thursday evening, *THEN* have a shower to save time in morning.

IF there is a walk to the bus stop, *THEN* leave an umbrella by the door in case it rains.

Example B: Improving home insulation

Improving home insulation could involve any number of changes, but it is too late once the winter comes round again and the heating is cranked up for another year.

Overall goal: To improve insulation in home

Breaking down the goal:

IF it is dusk, *THEN* close all the curtains in your house.

IF there is a draft coming under door, *THEN* write a note to buy a draft excluder on the weekend, and stick it on your notice board.

IF it is cold near to external doors, *THEN* fill unused keyholes with tissue paper.

Case study

One of the areas of sustainable behaviour that this kind of approach is most applicable to is travel behaviour and several campaigns have shown that focusing on the detail of complex goals like 'using public transport more often' is an effective way of achieving real results.

A few years ago in Australia, the government developed a programme called 'Travelsmart'. Thousands of people took part in the Travelsmart programme, and cut their carbon emissions by nearly 15%.

The programme worked so well because everyone who took part was provided with their own individualised travel plan.

This approach has since been taken up and adopted by the British Sustainable Transport charity Sustrans. Their work involves visiting people at home, reaching people at schools of in the workplace, and identifying exactly what their individual barriers and challenges to travelling more sustainably are. They then provide simple, motivating tools such as personalised maps, bus routes and information on safe walking and cycling paths.

An evaluation of 14 personalised travel plan initiatives across the UK found significant changes in travel behaviour, with an estimated saving of approximately 11.4 million car km a year.

Find out more

An evaluation of Sustrans's personalised travel plan initiatives
(http://www.sustrans.org.uk/assets/files/travelsmart/
dft_susttravel_pdf_040054.pdf)

Using planning to create new recycling habits at work
(http://www.goallab.nl/publications/documents/
Holland,%20Aarts,%20Langendam%20%282006%29%20-%20
implementation%20intentions%20on%20the%20workfloor.pdf)

CHAPTER 5

Using Scare Tactics: Does It Work?

What you need to know

CLIMATE CHANGE – AND THE CHALLENGE of getting to grips with sustainability – can seem daunting. But a lot of attempts at promoting sustainable behaviour fail because they simply make people feel guilty and don't inspire action. In a nutshell, studies on using fear (e.g. images of burning globes or starving children, or apocalyptic messages about destruction and despair) to motivate sustainable behaviour show that this approach has the potential to change attitudes towards the environment (for example, expressions of concern), but often not people's actions.

While fear of a negative outcome (e.g. lung cancer) can be an effective way of promoting behavioural changes (e.g. giving up smoking), the link between the threat and the behaviour must be personal and direct.

> *For most people in wealthy countries like the UK, climate change is perceived as neither a direct nor a personal threat and so shocking people into doing their recycling is not necessarily the right idea.*

One piece of research found that images that induced fear (such as environmental refugees or 'drowning' polar bears) were good for attracting attention, but ineffective at motivating genuine personal engagement (i.e. doing something about it!). Scaring people can work as a kind of 'spark' to generate awareness, but this must be coupled with constructive, practical information and support so that people can do something about it.

Un-threatening images that relate to people's everyday actions and concerns are more effective, and this links directly to work on using 'social norms' to promote sustainable behaviour (see Chapter 3). Showing people pictures of other people ('like them') engaging in meaningful sustainable behaviours (rather than scaring them with apocalyptic images) is likely to be a more productive way of motivating sustainable behaviour.

> *People need to know that other folk have also recognised the risks of climate change and that they are doing something about it.*

Another good strategy is to try and reduce the 'psychological distance' between people and climate change. Increased flooding is one of the impacts that scientists are very confident the UK will experience. Some research has looked, therefore, at the link between people's perceptions of climate change and whether or not they had suffered from flooding before. A study at Cardiff University[25] found that people who had experienced a flooding event were more likely to express concern over climate change and – crucially – to show a greater willingness to save energy to prevent the effects of climate change.

> *So linking individual experiences with climate change is one way of increasing the chance that people will want to do something about it.*

If you only do one thing...

If you want to raise awareness about the threat that the risks of climate change pose, try to do this using 'local' impacts. In the UK, there are a range of threats that climate change poses – none of them are catastrophic, but they are serious and people will be able to identify with them much more easily than talk of famine in sub-Saharan Africa. This short summary of how climate change will affect the UK (**http://webarchive. nationalarchives.gov.uk/20121015000000/www.direct.gov.uk/en/ Environmentandgreenerliving/Thewiderenvironment/Climatechange/ DG_072929**) may be useful. But don't just raise awareness of the risk – use the information in this book to explain concrete steps for doing something about it.

The theory that makes it work

For people who live in developed countries, climate change is mostly an 'invisible' threat, something that happens not here and not now. Although a changing climate will cause a range of problems for the UK – especially increased flooding and all the risks associated with it – it is difficult to point to locally relevant images or statistics that really capture the scale of the problem (at least for now). So, in order to show people in countries like the UK how bad climate change will be unless we move towards a more sustainable society, many early attempts at engaging the public by environmental charities or government agencies focused on finding ways of increasing the 'fear factor'. With pictures of starving African children, burning globes and drowning polar bears, the stereotypical imagery of climate change communication was born.

But research has now established that these images are not great ways of communicating climate change. For those who do not yet realise the potentially 'scary' aspects of climate change, people need to first experience themselves as vulnerable to the risks in some way in order to feel moved or affected.[25,26,27] The danger is that fear-inducing images and messages can be disempowering, producing feelings of helplessness, remoteness and lack of control.[28]

Unless carefully used in a message that contains constructive advice and a personal and direct link with the individual, fear is likely to trigger barriers to engagement with climate change, such as denial.[29,30] Similarly, studies have shown that guilt can play a role in motivating people to take action but can also function to stimulate defensive mechanisms against the perceived threat or challenge to people's sense of identity (as a good, moral person).

In fact, a study by psychologists at Berkeley, California[31] found that 'apocalyptic' messages about climate change impacted on different people in different ways. For those who believed in a 'just world' – that bad things don't, by and large, happen to good people – messages that ended in dire consequences actually increased their scepticism about climate change. The researchers suggested that the conflict between the negative impacts of climate change (happening to 'good people') and their belief in a just world led to the message being ignored, and even used as evidence that climate change was not occurring.

Putting the theory into practice

If you can identify a 'local' risk of climate change, and identify practical steps people can take to reduce that risk, then you will be using the threat of climate change in the way that is most likely to lead to behaviour change.

However, it is difficult to point to any definitive impacts of climate change that have *already* occurred. Increased flooding is one of the climate change impacts that the UK will have to face, but of course flooding happened before humans started to alter the climate.

So be careful not to overstate the link between climate change and extreme weather events like flooding. You can say that climate change makes these kinds of occurrences more likely to happen – it loads the dice – but it is not, on its own, responsible for every flood or heat wave that take place.

Case study

In 2009, the UK government launched a TV advertisement and series of newspaper adverts named 'Bedtime Stories', which were designed to engage the public on climate change. The TV advert depicted a young girl being read a scary story about climate change as cartoon sea levels rose around her house and spooky music played in the background. The story in the ad rather dramatically suggested that it was possible to 'save the land for the children' and showed a cartoon girl turning off her bedroom light, ending with the message: 'it's up to us how the story ends... see what you can do: search online for "ActOn CO2"'. The campaign was withdrawn following complaints to the Advertising Standards Authority about the newspaper ads, which were judged to have made too strong a link between flooding and climate change. But many people also criticised the TV advert on the basis that using scare tactics was not an especially good way of encouraging sustainable behaviour.

So what should it have said instead? The basic concept of a children's story is not necessarily a bad one, but as most people do not feel personally threatened by climate change, going for the scare tactics was not a good decision. Instead, the story could have focused on characters who worked together to share the challenge of creating a more sustainable society, presented images of ordinary, everyday people cycling to work, taking the train to go on holiday, or discussing ways of making their houses more heat-efficient with their neighbours.

Find out more

Avoid the Bedtime Stories approach
(http://www.youtube.com/watch? v=SDthR9RH0gw)

CHAPTER 6

Putting It All Together: Making Wider Change

THIS SHORT BOOK IS DESIGNED to provide practical – but crucially, evidence-based – guidance for promoting sustainable behaviour. By focusing on high-impact behaviours (Chapter 1), thinking about the values and sense of identity that underpin individual actions (Chapter 2), paying attention to the powerful influence of social norms and social networks (Chapter 3), using well-targeted strategies for breaking complex, habitual behaviours down into manageable chunks (Chapter 4) and avoiding the scare tactics and guilt-trips of so many environmental campaigns (Chapter 5), it is possible to design programmes for promoting sustainable behaviour that are meaningful, effective and have a measurable impact.

Following these principles will also provide the best chance of sustaining change over time. If a behaviour becomes defining for an individual (or even better their social group); if new, sustainable habits can be created; and if the sorts of values that go hand-in-hand with sustainable behaviour can be activated and nurtured, then sustainable behaviours won't simply disappear as soon as the financial incentive isn't there, or the initial interest subsides.

But even the best-designed campaign to promote sustainable behaviour is limited in its scope if it fails to link everyday behaviours to the wider challenges of sustainability. How can bridges between individual-level changes and community/social/political processes be made? What are the factors beyond behaviour change that anyone promoting sustainability should always have in the back of their mind? How does sustainable behaviour fit into the bigger picture?

Social networks

Chapter 3 began to answer the question of how to go beyond thinking about people as isolated individuals and harness the power of social norms. But the strategy of focusing on the 'social' rather than the 'individual' can be taken much further than asking people to make visible public commitments (e.g. a pledge on a car-share notice board), or spreading positive social norms by providing people with information about what their colleagues are doing.

Social networks (real, physical ones as well as online communities) are everywhere, and new behaviours spread through social networks like the ripples of a stone dropped into a pond.

Most people do not have a social network with sustainability at its core, but working to develop a group – rather than individual – sense of environmental responsibility and identity should be at the heart of any sustainability campaign. What is it that defines the group you are targeting and how can this identity be linked to sustainable behaviour?

The extent to which new behaviours spread though a social network depends on the number of 'social ties', but also on the strength of those ties.[32] Information is likely to spread quickly the more 'ties' there are in a network, but it is more likely to influence behaviour when it is received through strong ties (for example, a family member) than weak ones. So think about who is involved in promoting sustainable behaviour – is it a well-liked colleague with lots of strong social ties at work?

The idea that information and innovation can spread through social networks is not a new one. In the field of commercial marketing, advertising campaigns targeting 'opinion leaders' and influential individuals is commonplace. In other fields – health behaviour, for example – campaigns often target peer groups and existing social networks, in the hope that the spreading of positive health behaviours will be more likely within groups of individuals who trust each other and pay attention to each others' behaviour.

Targeting social networks also helps to enhance 'social capital' – something that is critical for building the resilience to cope with and adapt to changes brought about by adapting to climate change.[33] And the effectiveness of group-based programmes at promoting pro-environmental behaviour change has been demonstrated on numerous occasions – participants in these projects consistently point to a sense of mutual learning and support as a key reason for making and maintaining changes in behaviour.[34]

Social networks are important for creating a social identity that incorporates sustainability as a guiding principle,[35] rather than simply passing on a series of disjointed behaviours that may benefit the environment. If sustainable behaviour becomes *defining* for a social group, more significant behavioural changes (reinforced through peer pressure) are likely to be forthcoming.

Employers – reciprocal change

If you are promoting sustainable behaviour at work, then there is an obvious place that most workers would look to for leadership: their employer.

> *Changes in personal behaviour among workers can catalyse further changes from an employer because the argument that 'we've done our bit, now you do yours' is a powerful one.*

Also, if campaigns to promote sustainable behaviour are framed around the right kinds of values, they can help to generate a different type of workplace culture, one where it is normal to work co-operatively with others on issues like climate change and sustainability. However, while working co-operatively to reduce the carbon footprint of the organisation as a whole is clearly a must, there is nothing to say that a bit of friendly competition hurts either, as this example (**http://www.cloudapps.com/**) of a work-based sustainability tool shows.

Developed by a firm called CloudApps, the sustainability measuring and reporting system allows groups of colleagues to record their carbon use, and compete to see who can save the most energy. Drawing directly on research showing the importance of social norms and social networks for promoting sustainable behaviour, firms that have adopted the tool have shown considerable energy savings.

> *By taking advantage of the natural human desire to keep up with the Joneses, applications like this can kick-start a process of change that has a momentum all of its own.*

Many employers run formal car-share schemes, but if this is not yet in place where you work, then consider following a guide like one from **www.liftshare.com** and setting one up. Although it is written with employers in mind, it contains loads of useful tools for getting employers interested. It includes surveys that you (or your employer) can give to members of staff to gauge interest, as well as useful examples of what incentives other employers have offered to staff signing up to car share schemes at work (although remember that incentives should be linked to 'intrinsic' values as much as possible). But even if your employer won't go as far as establishing a formal car-share scheme, they may be able to provide incentives such as priority parking spaces for car-sharers.

> *Always consider how practical steps like these can be as well-informed as possible by the research evidence: foster positive social norms, break complex behaviours down into manageable chunks, and frame your messages around values that will catalyse more sustainable behaviours in the future.*

The Cycle to Work scheme is a national initiative run by the UK government, aimed at providing employees with tax-free bikes. Typical savings are between 30 and 50% of the price of a new bike. Employers can run the scheme themselves, or sign up with a third-party provider such as **www.cyclescheme.co.uk**. Employees then visit an approved bike shop, choose their bike and accessories, and arrange for the cost to be invoiced to the employer. The employee then 'hires' the bike from the employer through regular monthly instalments, until the bike is paid for, at which point they make a final payment and take permanent ownership of the bike.

The link between personal change and political change

There is a circular relationship between public views and the policies that politicians think are acceptable to support. Without the backing of the public, ambitious changes to the way our energy is supplied, or our transport system is structured, will never happen. But public views are to some extent shaped by the urgency with which the government and the media treat an issue. If politicians go quiet on climate change and sustainability, this sends a powerful signal that it is not a top priority.

So any campaign to promote sustainable behaviour in the workplace should try to make an explicit link between ordinary, everyday behaviours and government strategies for sustainability. One obvious way of doing this is to support Trade Union initiatives for 'green jobs', which argue that especially during tough economic times, investment in low-carbon employment is critical.

> *It is critical to ensure that focusing on individual behaviour changes does not become a diversion from the process of bringing political pressure to bear on policy-makers, and the importance of public demonstrations of frustration at both the lack of political progress on sustainability and the barriers presented by vested interests should not be underestimated.*

There is no reason that developing messages about sustainable behaviour should be detached from the political context, and communicating about sustainability can play a role in fostering demand for – as well as acceptance of – policy change.[36]

Focusing on sustainable behaviour in the workplace is also a very good way of identifying all the structural barriers to behaviour change, such as the cost of public transport or the lack of safe cycling lanes. These are not issues that any one individual – or even an entire organisation – could do much about. But if a group of people can show that they have done everything within their power to move towards sustainability, and there are still barriers in the way, then this is a powerful argument to persuade local and national policy-makers to take action.

However, there is one more important reason why promoting sustainable behaviour should never be detached from the politics of sustainability. How people act says something about their underlying values, the priorities they hold, and the type of world they want to live in. It may have become a tired old cliché, but 'being the change you want to see' still sends out an important message. If done right, promoting sustainable behaviour can mean so much more than a clever slogan or an appeal for people to 'do their bit' – it can be a political act in itself.

Conclusion

THE IDEA THAT WE NEED TO WORK towards a more sustainable society is no longer a fringe position. It is only going to become more important over the coming years and decades. Promoting sustainable behaviour is not easy, but armed with the best evidence and practical advice it is possible to make meaningful, measurable, and long-lasting changes in people's behaviour at home and in the workplace.

> *If there is one message to take away from this book, it is that individuals – and individual behaviours – cannot be separated from their social context.*

We act according to our personal values and priorities and in line with the social norms of our peer group, whereupon much of our everyday behaviour becomes habitual and difficult to change. Focus on linking specific behaviours with underlying values, understand that people look to others around them for cues about what to do, and try not to become too bogged down with actions that have a limited payoff in terms of sustainability.

The social science research presented in this book gives you signposts and educated guidance, but because humans are not machines, it doesn't give you guarantees. It tells you how people *tend* to behave and respond, but there is no substitute for having an in-depth understanding of the audience you are working with. So this book provides you – the catalyst

CONCLUSION

for change – with the tools you need, not the finished product. It may seem an uphill struggle at times. But there is a critical role for people's everyday behaviour to play in the transition towards sustainability.

....

Mapping Principles to Case Studies

Principle for promoting sustainable behaviour	Where is this being applied
Focus on 'intrinsic' values	The website **www.valuesandframes.org** shows how organisations from the private, public and charity sectors are framing their messages about sustainability using values that make a sustainable society more likely in the long run.
Harness the power of social norms	The energy company Opower (**www.opower. com**) is transforming the way people receive their energy bills by applying the latest thinking on social norms.
Create sustainable habits	Before you can change a habit, you need to break it down into bite-size chunks. Sustrans's (**www.sustrans.org.uk**) 'Travelsmart' programme identifies individual barriers and challenges to travelling more sustainably and provides simple, motivating tools such as personalised maps, bus routes and information on safe walking and cycling paths.

Avoid scare tactics	Learn from the government's mistakes. Watch the Bedtime Stories advert (**http://www.youtube.com/watch? v=SDthR9RHOgw**), and don't promote your campaign for sustainable behaviour by showing scared kids and cartoon floods.
Tap into social competition in the workplace	The success of the CloudApps (**www.cloudapps.com**) software in some big organisations shows that tapping into social norms and social networks – and the natural competitiveness that we all possess – can lead to big carbon savings.

Promoting Sustainable Behaviour – The People and Projects That You Need to Know About

THERE ARE NOW SEVERAL GROUPS and organisations doing good work on sustainable behaviour, as well as some excellent online resources. The 'Green Living' blog (**http://greenallianceblog.org.uk/category/ behaviour-change/**), an initiative of Green Alliance (**http://www.green-alliance.org.uk/home/**), is a good place to explore in more depth debates about how best to promote sustainable behaviour. The website 'Talking Climate' (**http://www.talkingclimate.org**, edited by the author of this book) offers a gateway to new research on climate change communication, and regular blogs from leading academics in the field.

In terms of practical projects, there are several third-sector organisations which do good work on sustainable behaviour. Sustrans (**http:// www.sustrans.org.uk**) is a charity that focuses on promoting more sustainable transport behaviour, using evidence from research studies to inform its programmes, while the charity Global Action Plan (**http:// www.globalactionplan.org.uk/**) describes itself as the UK's 'leading environmental behaviour change charity', and has initiated and led lots of projects aimed at generating lasting behavioural changes in community and work-based groups.

Although different political parties have different ideas about whether they 'do' behaviour change or not, the current government houses a Behavioural Insights Team (**http://www.cabinetoffice.gov.uk/behavioural-insights-team**), which has produced a report on behaviour change and energy use. Under new legislation launched in 2012 (known as the 'Green Deal' – **http://www.decc.gov.uk/en/content/cms/tackling/green_deal/green_deal.aspx**), the government is aiming to install insulation in 14 million households by 2020, and provide millions of 'smart meters' that will help people monitor their energy use. The success of the Green Deal will hinge on whether people buy into it and so this is a huge opportunity for incorporating evidence on how to promote sustainable behaviour effectively.

References

1. Druckman, A., Chitnisa, M., Sorrell, S. and Jackson, T. 2011. Missing carbon reductions? Exploring rebound and backfire effects in UK households. *Energy Policy* (Volume 39): 3572–3581.

2. Vlek, C., Rothengatter, T., Steg, L. and Abrahamse, W. 2005. A review of intervention studies aimed at household energy conservation. *Journal of Environmental Psychology* (Volume 25 Issue 3): 273–291.

3. Thøgersen, J. and Crompton, T. 2009. Simple and painless? The limitations of spillover in environmental campaigning. *Journal of Consumer Policy* (Volume 32): 141–163.

4. Spence, A. and Pidgeon, N.F. 2009. Psychology, climate change and sustainable behavior. *Environment: Science and Policy for Sustainable Development* (Volume 6): 8–18.

5. Berners-Lee, M. 2010. *How Bad are Bananas? The Carbon Footprint of Everything* (London: Profile Books Ltd).

6. Gardner, G. and Stern, P. 2009. The short list: The most effective actions U.S. households can take to curb climate change. *Environment*, December, 2009.

7. Schwartz, S.H. 1992. Universals in the content and structure of values: Theoretical advances and empirical tests in 20 countries. In: Zanna, M.P. (Ed.) *Advances in Experimental Social Psychology*, vol. 25 (San Diego, CA: Academic Press), pp. 1– 65.

8. Stern, P.C. 2000. Towards a coherent theory of environmentally significant behavior. *Journal of Social Issues* (Volume 56): 407–424.

9. Slimak, M.W. and Dietz, T. 2006. Personal values, beliefs, and ecological risk perception. *Risk Analysis* (Volume 26): 1689–1705.

REFERENCES

10. Dunlap, R.E., Grieneeks, J.K. and Rokeach, M., 1983. Human values and pro-environmental behaviour. In: Conn, W.D. (Ed.) *Energy and Material Resources: Attitudes, Values, and Public Policy* (Boulder, CO: Westview Press).

11. Nilsson, A., von Borgstede, C. and Biel, A. 2004. Willingness to accept climate change strategies: The effect of values and norms. *Journal of Environmental Psychology* (Volume 24): 267–277.

12. Dobson, A. 2010. *Environmental Citizenship and Pro-environmental Behaviour: Rapid Research and Evidence Review* (London: Sustainable Development Research Network).

13. Whitmarsh, L. and O'Neill, S. 2010. Green identity, green living? The role of pro-environmental self-identity in determining consistency across diverse pro-environmental behaviours. *Journal of Environmental Psychology* (Volume 30): 305–314.

14. Evans, L., Maio, G., Corner, A., Hodgetts, C.J., Ahmed, S. and Hahn, U. 2012. Self interest and pro-environmental behaviour. *Nature Climate Change*. doi: 10.1038/NCLIMATE1662.

15. Lakoff, G., 2004. *Don't Think of an Elephant! Know Your Values and Frame the Debate* (White River Junction, VT: Chelsea Green Publishing).

16. Crompton, T. 2010. *Common Cause: The Case for Working with Our Cultural Values* (Godalming, Surrey: WWF UK).

17. Schultz, P.W., Nolan, J.M., Cialdini, R.B., Goldstein, N.J. and Griskevicius, V. 2007. The constructive, destructive, and reconstructive power of social norms. *Psychological Science* (Volume 18 Issue 5): 429–434.

18. Cialdini, R.B. 2003. Crafting normative messages to protect the environment. *Current Directions in Psychological Science* (Volume 12 Issue 4): 105–109.

19. Allcott, H. 2011. Social norms and energy conservation. *Journal of Public Economics* (Volume 95, 1082–1095).

20. Gollwitzer, P.M. 1999. Implementation intentions: Strong effects of simple plans. *American Psychologist* (Volume 54): 493–503.

21. Elliot, M.A. and Armitage, C.J. 2006. Effects of implementations on the self-reported frequency of drivers' compliance with speed limits. *Journal of Experimental Psychology: Applied* (Volume 12): 108–117.

22. Verplanken, B. and Wood, W. 2006. Interventions to break and create consumer habits. *Journal of Public Policy and Marketing* (Volume 25): 90–103.

23. Holland, R.W., Aarts, H. and Langendam, D. 2006. Breaking and creating habits on the working floor: A field-experiment on the power of implementation intentions. *Journal of Experimental Social Psychology* (Volume 42): 776–783.

24. Bamberg, S. 2002. Effects of implementation intentions on the actual performance of new environmentally friendly behaviours – results of two field experiments. *Journal of Environmental Psychology* (Volume 22): 399–411.

25. Spence, A., Poortinga, W., Butler, C. and Pidgeon, N. 2011. Perceptions of climate change and willingness to save energy related to flood experience. *Nature Climate Change* (Volume 1 Issue 1): 46–49.

26. Das, E.H.H.J., de Wit, J.B.F. and Stroebe, W. 2003. Fear appeals motivate acceptance of action recommendations: Evidence for a positive bias in the processing of persuasive messages. *Personality and Social Psychology Bulletin* (Volume 29): 650–664

27. Hoog, N., Stroebe, W. and de Wit, J.B.F. 2005. The impact of fear appeals on processing and acceptance of action recommendations. *Personality & Social Psychology Bulletin* (Volume 31): 24–33.

28. O'Neill, S. and Nicholson-Cole, S. 2009. 'Fear won't do it': Promoting positive engagement with climate change through visual and iconic representations. *Science Communication* (Volume 30): 355–379.

29. Stoll-Kleemann, S., O'Riordan, T. and Jaeger, C.C. 2001. The psychology of denial concerning climate mitigation measures: Evidence from Swiss focus groups. *Global Environmental Change* (Volume 11 Issue 2): 107–117.

30. Lorenzoni, I., Nicholson-Cole, S. and Whitmarsh, L. 2007. Barriers perceived to engaging with climate change among the UK public and their policy implications. *Global Environmental Change* (Volume 17 Issue 3–4): 445–459.

REFERENCES

31. Feinberg, M. and Willer, R. 2010. Apocalypse soon? Dire messages reduce belief in global warming by contradicting just-world beliefs. *Psychological Science* (Volume 22 Issue 1): 34–38.

32. Granovetter, M.S. 1973. The strength of weak ties. *American Journal of Sociology* (Volume 78): 1360–1380.

33. Rowson, J., Broome, S. and Jones, A. 2010. *Connected Communities: How Social Networks Power and Sustain the Big Society* (London: Royal Society of Arts).

34. Nye, M. and Burgess, J. 2008. *Promoting Durable Change in Household Waste and Energy Use Behaviour* (London: Department for Environment, Food & Rural Affairs, UK).

35. Rabinovich, A., Morton, T.A. and Duke, C.C. 2010. Collective self and individual choice: The role of social comparisons in promoting climate change. In: Whitmarsh, L., O'Neill, S. and Lorenzoni, I. (Eds) *Engaging the Public with Climate Change: Behaviour Change and Communication* (London: Earthscan).

36. Ockwell, D., O'Neill, S. and Whitmarsh, L. 2009. Reorienting climate change communication for effective mitigation: Forcing people to be green or fostering grass-roots engagement? *Science Communication* (Volume 30): 305–327.

....

Green Jujitsu:

The Smart Way to Embed Sustainability into Your Organisation

Gareth Kane

Terra Infirma Ltd, gareth@terrainfirma.co.uk

Abstract

BUSINESS HAS RECENTLY WOKEN UP to the need to address environmental sustainability in a meaningful way. No longer is it sufficient to have an environmental policy or environmental management system – substantial changes to business practice are required. Culture change is widely regarded as the most vital and the most difficult element of this paradigm shift. The standard methods of 'switch it off' stickers, awareness presentations and proclamations from the top have proved incapable of delivering the shift in attitudes required. Green Jujitsu is a completely different way of looking at culture change for environmental sustainability. Instead of trying to correct your colleagues' perceived 'weaknesses', it focuses instead on playing to their strengths to get them truly interested and engaged. This principle is applied to the 'elephant model' of culture change: providing clear guidance, inspiring people emotionally and altering the working environment. These techniques are illustrated with case studies from the author's own experience of facilitating culture change on the front line in some of the world's leading organisations.

About The Author

GARETH KANE is an internationally recognised environmental and sustainability expert. He has appeared as a media pundit on sustainability issues on, for example, the BBC Six O'Clock News, Countryfile, The Politics Show and local radio. In 2008 The Journal newspaper named Gareth as a 'Rising Star, Future Leader' for his work on sustainability.

Gareth's consultancy Terra Infirma has a client list including the BBC, BAE Systems plc, Johnson Matthey plc, the NHS and East Coast Mainline. In June 2010 the company was singled out for praise in the press by UK Environment Secretary, the Rt Hon Caroline Spelman MP. Terra Infirma's Green Academy online training programme has attracted participants from around the globe – from the USA to New Zealand.

Gareth was elected onto Newcastle City Council in 2004. Until 2011, he was deputy Executive Member for Environment and Sustainability which culminated in Newcastle being declared the UK's most sustainable city by Forum for the Future in 2009 and 2010. He is now opposition spokesman on Sustainability.

Gareth is the author of two books on business and sustainability, most recently *The Green Executive*.

What Is The Biggest Barrier To Corporate Sustainability?

THIS IS A QUESTION I AM OFTEN ASKED from the floor at speaking engagements. My answer is a little trite but very true: 'The biggest barrier is only six inches wide – it's the space between our ears.'

The root cause of much unsustainable practice is *attitude* – lack of priority, busy-ness, ignorance, habit, short-sightedness, despondence, fear, laziness or combinations of the above. Bad attitude seems to get worse exponentially with the size of the business – sustainable energy expert Amory Lovins has said that while 'primitive' animals like ants have communities which exhibit intelligence way beyond that of the sum of the individuals, the more humans you group together, the more stupid their combined behaviour[1].

When we think about environmental sustainability we tend to envision shiny new technology such as solar panels and electric vehicles. However, it has been estimated that 60–70% of internal environmental improvements are dependent on getting staff to change their behaviour[2]. When I visit clients it is all too common to see heating and air-conditioning switched on at the same time, hosepipes left running but stuck down a drain, valuable packaged products damaged by forklift trucks and potentially green technologies like teleconferencing facilities gathering dust. And beyond that, more substantial environmental improvements such as redesigning products and greening the supply chain depend on a proper culture of sustainability integrated throughout the organisation.

Changing the culture of an organisation is one of the key management challenges. When it is done correctly, the results can be dramatic. The uptake of Total Quality Management (TQM) in Japan has led to the country leading in the motor vehicle and photographic/optical equipment sectors, despite having no natural resources and very high labour costs. One of the key planks of TQM is that quality becomes everyone's responsibility – it needs to be embedded into the organisation.

Figure 1 shows my sustainability maturity model for organisations.

....

FIGURE 1. Sustainability maturity model.

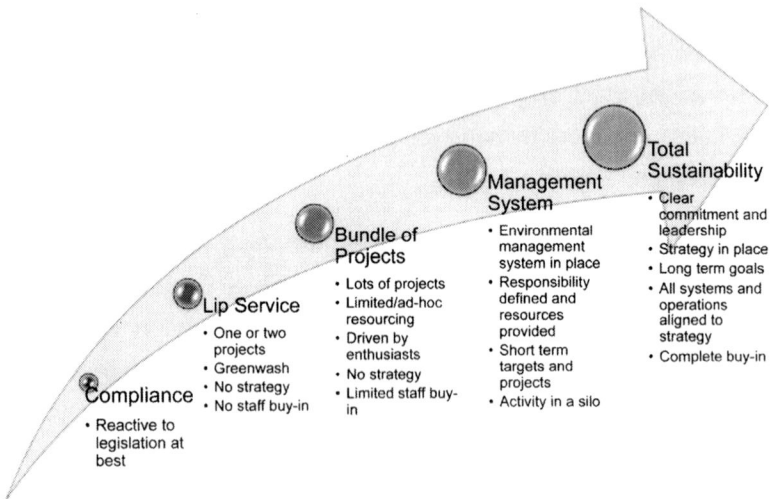

....

72

The stages are largely self-explanatory and the challenge for most organisations is to make the leap from the 'Management Systems' level, where environmental issues are 'managed' in a green silo, up to 'Total Sustainability' where sustainability is embedded into the organisation.

One of the biggest differences between the top two levels is making sustainability everyone's responsibility – just like quality under TQM. This manifests itself in the attitude of employees. I can tell very quickly which businesses 'get it' and which don't by a few conversations with staff members.

However, this is one area where many organisations struggle – culture change is very difficult and many simply try 'me-too' solutions such as awareness posters and environmental champions without properly thinking through what has to be done. This e-book proposes a smarter way of approaching culture change, bringing people along with you and playing to their strengths rather than trying to browbeat them into submission. There is a parallel here between boxing and jujitsu – in the former you try to overpower your opponent, in the latter you use people's strengths to get them where you want them. We will be considering this analogy in more detail in Chapter 2, but first we will look at problems faced by most conventional environmental sustainability programmes.

. . . .

CHAPTER 1

Why Sustainability Programmes Fail

What's the problem?

I DIAGNOSE THE MOST COMMON BARRIERS in environmental sustainability programmes as:

- Lack of leadership: leadership is critical to any successful corporate programme and a lack of leadership will kill off culture change programmes before they get going.

- A lack of integration: 'green' and 'sustainability' are seen as tangential issues to the mainstream business processes and are thus of secondary importance or someone else's problem.

- A misalignment of responsibility and authority: most environmental managers have lots of responsibility and precious little authority. Conversely, people who have the power to push sustainability are given no responsibility to do so.

- A lack of accountability: environmental performance is left outside the performance management system.

- Wishful or limited thinking: 'We've appointed energy champions. Job done.'

- Sloppy company culture in general: I find that the companies who have a poor sustainability culture usually have poor discipline, weak quality standards and messy premises.

- A lack of empowerment: 'It's more than my job's worth to turn that off.'

- Ignorance: 'If I turn up the thermostat, the office will warm more quickly.'

- Inertia: 'We've always designed our products like that.' 'That sound? That's always there. No, we don't check our compressed air system for leaks. Should we?', etc.

- Fear: 'If we try this, who'll get the blame if it goes wrong?'

You will notice that these are predominantly about attitude and culture – very rarely is the real reason money. Northern Foods have saved many millions of pounds in energy and waste costs and they say 60–70% of it was achieved through low or no-cost behavioural changes[2].

I say again that the true barrier to sustainability is about six inches wide – the space between our ears. Most of the problems and solutions can be found there.

Why 'switch it off' doesn't work

The traditional approach to behavioural change has been to slather 'switch it off' stickers and posters over every switch, wall and machine. If culture change was that easy, you wouldn't be reading this e-book.

I once worked with a company which had A3 posters on sustainability in every hallway and foyer. Each sheet was packed with text on company policy. As an experiment I asked one workshop contingent whether they knew the company's definition of sustainability. No-one did. I asked if anyone had read the statement. No-one had. There was nothing in this communication to encourage anyone to read. It was a complete waste of time and effort.

So why doesn't it work?

- The injunctions to act get lost amongst the noise of the multitude of messages we are bombarded with every day.

- People generally resent being hectored and may resist as a reflex reaction.

- There's no explanation of the benefits of this action either to the individual, the business or wider society.

- Familiarity breeds contempt – you soon stop noticing the signs and posters.

- The message is usually uninspiring, lifeless and dull.

At best, these programmes are launched because of a lack of imagination. At worst, they are for the ego of the originator rather than the intended audience. A prime suspect is the ubiquitous 'Please consider the impact on the environment before printing this email' line in email signature blocks, which is clearly there to say 'I think I'm morally superior to you.'

Institutional inertia

I have already quoted Amory Lovins saying that animals like ants have communities which exhibit intelligence way beyond that of the sum of the individuals, but the more humans you group together, the more stupid the combined behaviour (or words to that effect). As an optimist, I like to think of this phenomenon as 'institutional inertia' rather than group stupidity. My definition of institutional inertia is:

> *The more people you get together,*
> *the harder it is to effect change.*

You can see this if you go on holiday with a group of friends and try to decide which restaurant to eat at one evening. The length of time it takes to make the decision and act increases exponentially with the number of people involved. If you are a couple, you'll probably be onto your coffee before a group of eight has sat down.

When you scale this up to the organisational level a huge number of factors kick in: internal politics, factionalism, fear of failure, fear to speak up, fear of standing out, the desire to belong, tradition (aka 'the way it's done round here'), formal and informal hierarchies, etc., etc. – they all add up to considerable inertia.

The challenge of overcoming this inertia – 'turning the supertanker around' – is immense. In my experience, the most important factors are strong, consistent leadership and a somewhat counter-intuitive combination of bone-headed determination and nimble culture change techniques. This e-book will help you with the latter, but the others have to come from within.

How not to do culture change

There are a number of pitfalls that many people fall into when trying to change the culture in organisations:

- Preaching: preaching doesn't work. It is as simple as that. The temptation to preach is very strong, in particular amongst those of us who feel very strongly about environmental issues. But it is counter-productive and simply switches people off.

- Irrelevance: talking about the plight of the polar bear or orang-utan may get people's sympathy, but both are too far removed from the everyday experience of your staff to make them want to change the way they behave. In general, in my sessions I only mention the scale of environmental impacts in passing to put solutions in context.

- Eco-clichés: despite my long campaign against them, there is still a prevalence of eco-clichés in imagery in green messages. Pictures of hands cupping saplings make me want to scream and they send out the subconscious message 'here's the worthy but dull bit, normal service will continue shortly'.

- Not getting leadership fully signed up: leadership is a key plank of culture change. Unfortunately, many CEOs are scared of the sustainability agenda and have a tendency to disappear whenever the topic is debated.

- Unintended consequences of incentives: take care with financial incentives as they can produce all sorts of unintended consequences and it is possible to stir up resentment accidentally. Some issues, for example, staff parking, raise passions way beyond what they logically should.

- Not realigning other systems such as human resources policies so they promote a more sustainable culture. We will look at this in more detail in Chapters 5 and 6.

- Taking your foot off the pedal: the secret of success in fostering green behaviour is to keep going.

- Cognitive dissonance: this occurs when we try and hold two conflicting ideas in our heads at the same time. For example, if you try to foster a culture where sustainability is strong, then ask employees to take clearly unsustainable actions, they will get confused and cynical.

Questions for you

How would you rate your culture of sustainability from 1–5, where 1 means no culture at all and 5 means everyone understands what sustainability means to them?

Why do you rate the company like this?

What tone does your sustainability programme currently take?

How relevant is it to the day-to-day activities of your employees?

CHAPTER 2

The Green Jujitsu Approach

The jujitsu analogy

SO, GIVEN THAT WE HAVE SEEN that culture change for sustainability is very difficult, how do we make sustainability stick? The answer is to harness the strengths of your employees rather than focusing on their weaknesses.

The analogy that spans this e-book is the difference between boxing and the martial art of jujitsu. Boxing involves standing toe to toe with your opponent and trying to batter the living daylights out of them – before they do the same to you. Such a war of attrition will be familiar to many, if not all, sustainability practitioners.

Jujitsu, however, is about using your opponent's strength, energy and momentum against them and levering them into submission. I'm not going to stretch the analogy too thin – there is no deeper philosophical or technical similarity between embedding sustainability and a martial art – in fact, seeing your employees as 'opponents' won't do your efforts much good. But the idea of bringing people with you by understanding their strengths and weaknesses is an extremely powerful one as we shall see.

In the rest of this e-book, we will be considering this approach to embedding environmental sustainability into the culture of the organisation. Simple changes, such as changing a statement into a question, can increase your likelihood of success by a remarkable degree.

Understanding attitudes to sustainability

Attitudes towards the environment and concepts such as sustainable development vary across a wide spectrum. As in any relationship, it is important to understand the other party's point of view or 'where they are coming from' to build mutual respect. Conversely, completely

. . . .

FIGURE 2. Attitudes to the environment and sustainability.

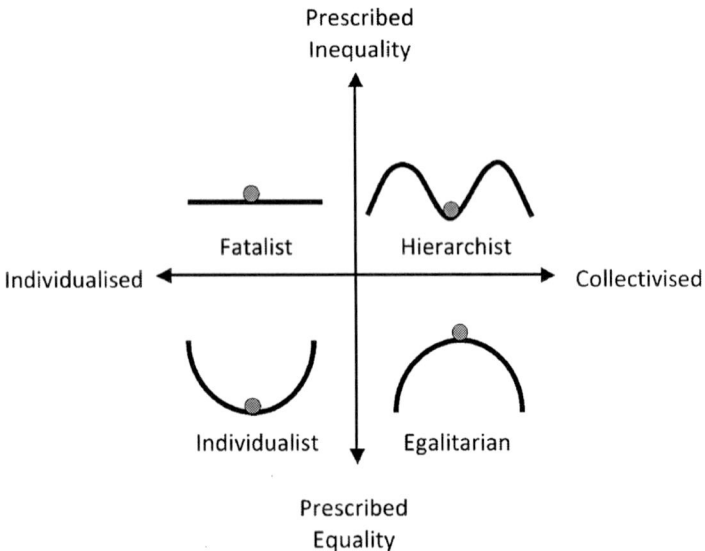

SOURCE: Adapted from Thompson, M., Ellis, R. and Widavsky, A. 1990. *Cultural Theory* (Boulder, CO: Westview Press).

. . . .

different attitudes to the same problem or issue often cause conflict and rancour. So it is worth considering different attitudes to environmental sustainability.

Many social scientists use the model in Figure 2 to categorise attitudes to society and nature[3], each attitude being defined by the degree of equality/inequality and individualism/collectivism. The model uses a red ball representing the state of the environment on a surface. If the red ball is moved a small amount (an environmental impact), then it will either stay where it is (another stable state), return to its original position (resilient to change), or drop off the model (ecological breakdown).

The four attitudes are:

1. Individualists believe that the planet is robust and there to be exploited. This is the typical belief of free marketeers and so-called 'climate change deniers'.

2. Hierarchists believe the environment is there to be exploited within limits. This is the typical approach of governments and public sector bodies.

3. Egalitarians believe that the environment is fragile and requires protection. Environmental damage must be minimised at all costs. Typical approach of environmental pressure groups.

4. Fatalists don't have a view on whether any state of the environment is better or worse on any other state – the whole debate passes them by.

These are caricatures of course, but they help explain why, say, if you present a randomly selected group of people with analytical data on an environmental problem such as climate change, some will accept it (hierarchists), some will say it is exaggerated (individualists), some will say you aren't taking the risk seriously enough (egalitarians) and others will simply shrug (fatalists).

Internal resistance

The jujitsu approach requires us to understand and overcome resistance to sustainability. Resistance to sustainability from individuals can come in a number of forms:

- Anti-green sentiments: as we saw above, many people (individualists) find the idea of natural limits is anathema to their world view and, at worst, some pernicious form of communism in disguise.

- Narrow economic focus: 'sustainability is not a business issue and should be left to politicians'. This tends to go hand in hand with the individualist approach above.

- 'Too busy/not my problem': this is often a problem in middle management where individuals have many competing requirements for their attention.

- Limited ambition: 'OK, we've got ISO14001 certification, what more do you want?'

- Fear for the future: sustainability requires new ways of working which in turn requires risk taking. Many people are highly risk averse and resist change for the sake of it, but others may fear that their skills will become redundant in the new regime.

- Staff/management friction: staff members and/or their unions may believe that sustainability programmes will benefit the managerial classes but not people at the front line.

To use the jujitsu approach we have to recognise and understand these, while never accepting them as permanent obstacles. They can be overcome.

Motivations of different roles

Different job roles bring with them different priorities which must also be taken into consideration, for example:

- Boardroom/senior management: concerned with strategic opportunities and risks, brand protection and competitive advantage.

- Middle management: concerned with meeting short-/medium-term targets, delivering individual projects and managing costs. People at this level are often very aware of their own career prospects.

- Frontline staff: often detached from the corporate core in larger organisations. Their loyalty often lies with their immediate team rather than the organisation as a whole.

In addition, different types of staff will respond to different forms of information and approaches, for example:

- Technical staff: comfortable with data, graphs and charts – and will always want to see such evidence before acting. Give them a problem and they will want to find a solution.

- Financial staff: will respond best to financial data and cost/benefit analyses.

- Administrative staff: often ask 'how is this relevant to me?' A key strategy is to use human interest stories (see Chapter 3).

So if you want to engage frontline non-technical staff and senior financial directors, you will need to take quite different approaches.

The elephant model of culture change

My favoured model for the art of culture change uses the analogy of an elephant guided by a human rider walking along a path and was popularised by Dan and Chip Heath[4]. The direction the elephant takes is determined by three things: instructions provided to the elephant by the rider, the desires of the elephant itself and the nature of the path. The elements translate as:

- The rider is the logical, conscious part of our minds.

- The elephant is our subconscious – which is usually the strongest influence on our behaviour whether we like it or not.

- The path is the environment we operate in, with easier and more difficult routes, and distractions along the way.

To change the direction the elephant is travelling, we must provide clear instructions to the rider, engage emotionally with the elephant, and shape the path to 'nudge' people into following desired behaviour patterns. The following sections demonstrate how to apply the Green Jujitsu concept to each of these three culture change elements.

No pain, no gain

We mentioned in the last chapter that a common pitfall was to take your foot off the gas and assume the job has been done in one pass. When learning any martial art, part of the process is to repeat physical movements until they become instinctive. In the same way, you must train yourself and your organisation again and again until sustainability becomes instinctive. But even if you get to black belt in a martial art, if you stop training you will slowly lose the reflexes and fitness that got you there. Likewise with culture change, the new culture must be constantly reinforced to keep it as the predominant way of doing things.

Questions for you

Who are you trying to engage with?

What role(s) do they perform in the organisation?

What might put them off the sustainability agenda?

What turns them on?

CHAPTER 3

Providing Information

THE FIRST ELEMENT OF THE ELEPHANT MODEL of culture change is how to effectively communicate information to the rider and thus to the elephant. We have seen in Chapter 1 that most organisations find it very difficult to do this properly – the ubiquitous 'switch it off' sticker has failed to make an impact and they often struggle to know what to do next. Under the Green Jujitsu approach we need to think very carefully about the audience and tailor the message to appeal to them.

Fighting for attention

The main problem with giving instructions is information overload. Check out the notice board of any organisation and you will see 'death by poster' – 101 different instructions on everything from health and safety to the latest charity fundraising all desperately clamouring for the attention of passers-by. Add a poster on sustainability and it just becomes another voice lost in the babble.

A number of tactics are often used to get the message heard:

- Shock tactics: UK military bases used to use images of scantily clad women tripping on hazards to attract the attention of servicemen to health and safety messages. Such imagery is unacceptable by modern standards and in any case soon loses its impact.

- Guerrilla marketing: get your message posted in places where it is unexpected and you get a captive audience – for example, on the back of a toilet cubicle door.

- Interrupt your audience: a number of online marketing ventures involve an advert being played before a video or before an online article – again this can lead to annoying people rather than inspiring them.

Whichever approach you take, all you are doing is trying to shout louder than everyone else in a room full of people shouting. The Green Jujitsu approach doesn't require volume, but tailors the message so the audience wants to listen to it.

What is relevant to your audience?

So we need a message which is clear, concise and relevant to the audience. A vital pre-requisite is to find out what makes the audience tick and then package the message appropriately.

For example, my friend and colleague Graeme Mills of GPM Network was given the task of persuading employees of a regeneration charity to switch their computers off at night. When Graeme ran some focus groups, he found that those employees were so focused on their worthy projects, they tended to see other issues as a distraction. Graeme decided to tap into this narrow focus and developed a campaign where the PC screensavers told them 'if you switch off this computer every night, it saves the equivalent of making a £57 annual donation to our projects'. To employees, this was a significant personal donation, so switching off became a painless way to contribute to frontline projects.

Speaking their language

Another key Green Jujitsu tactic is to match your language to the audience. Words such as 'carbon', 'environment' or 'green' can lead to people either reacting badly if they are anti-green or simply switching off if they don't see the relevance. Words like 'energy', 'waste' and 'risk' can be more powerful to the ears of the unconverted – and after all, those are the people you need to speak to. Table 1 has some suggestions of 'green language' that you might want to avoid for certain audiences and some 'jujitsu' alternatives that sometimes work better.

TABLE 1: Green and Jujitsu Language

Green language	Jujitsu language
Green	Waste
The environment	Energy efficiency
The planet	Resource efficiency
Sustainable development	Lean manufacturing
Sustainability	Productivity
Climate change	Return on investment
Global warming	Legislation
Carbon emissions	Pollution
Carbon footprint	Liabilities
Corporate social responsibility	Risk
Community	Energy security
	Costs and savings
	Product differentiation
	Market opportunity
	Hazardous
	Health & safety

Use questions, not statements

Bold statements of fact to a cynic or sceptic can be like a red rag to a bull. Others will simply ignore statements if they think the problem is irrelevant or too difficult. In contrast, asking questions (maybe with a fact embedded in the middle) tends to give you momentum, as questions are less threatening and your opponent has to respond thoughtfully[5].

I use this frequently in my workshops. I normally start each session with the question 'Why should your company be concerned about sustainability?' This throws the responsibility for arguing the business case onto the audience, forcing them to work it out for themselves. This is much more effective than me, a stranger, trying to persuade them they should be concerned.

The same approach can be taken day to day in meetings, for example:

- 'Our biggest customer has issued a press release saying they want to address the carbon footprint of their supply chain – how do we respond?'

- 'How robust is the business to rising oil prices?'

- 'Do you know that we are wasting £2,000,000 on energy every year?'

- 'How are we going to respond to the EU's latest product stewardship legislation?'

This approach is particularly effective with senior management, who often prefer to be consulted on their views rather than being presented with a *fait accompli.*

Reframing the argument

A common mistake is to rush into a debate where the 'frame' of the argument is working against you. Like a window frame restricting the view outside a room, the 'frame' of an argument restricts the scope of the debate. We often plunge into an argument using the default frame which may stack the odds against us. Instead it is important to step back, consider the big picture and choose the 'correct' frame.

For example, if you find yourself debating 'environment *or* profit' with a senior manager, you are unlikely to make much headway. Rather than trying to fight that battle, you need to reframe the discussion as 'environment *and* profit', and then you will find barriers starting to fall as your aims and the interests of the manager are aligned.

Reframing arguments often involves starting discussions correctly. If you ask 'Should we be tackling sustainability issues?', you are giving the other person permission to answer 'No!' If, however, you ask 'How should we go about tackling sustainability?', the frame has shifted to obscure that answer, making it much more difficult to be so negative.

Effective switch it off

While I have been dismissive of 'switch it off' labels, there is a role for such instructions if you flip the approach around. Instead of saying 'you must switch this off', you say 'you may switch this off, but not that'.

A good example of this has been developed by Northern Foods – an £1 billion a year producer of ready meals. The system uses a three-colour labelling scheme on all factory equipment. A red label means 'leave it on, whatever'; green means 'if this machine doesn't appear to be doing anything useful, switch it off'; and amber means 'if you think this machine should be switched off, check with your supervisor'. This clear and empowering system is easy for a low skilled workforce, many of whom do not have English as a first (or sometimes second) language.

Feedback

When I graduated from college, I lived in a dingy bedsit in London for the first winter until I could afford something better. The room had an old-style spinning disk electricity meter by the door, so every time I switched on the electric cooker or the electric fire, the disk would start spinning like mad. I remember this visual feedback of how fast my money was disappearing making me use those appliances very carefully (I found that making pasta or rice warmed the room better than the heater, so I used to cook as soon as I got in from work). It has been found that people with meters that provide them with feedback on electricity consumption use 4% less than they would without[6].

Feedback has long been used by industry to influence behaviour in many aspects of performance. Many factories display the time since the last accident by the gate and many display ranks of bar charts covering everything from quality pass/fail rates to staff absences.

Some companies who have advanced energy management system use real-time feedback. One example is a simple traffic light system to show if consumption is low (green), high (amber) or very high (red). This is a nice way of converting data into a form that staff can easily grasp and of course you can tighten the amber and red settings to encourage continual improvement.

Storytelling

If you look at any newsagent's shelf, many of the magazines will be dominated by true-life stories and personalities. If you switch on the TV news, no matter what the news item is, they will inevitably turn to someone affected for their views, no matter how tangential or inconsequential. Why? Because we like to hear stories from 'people like us'. Converting the message into a personal story is a powerful way of making it more engaging.

At defence giant BAE Systems plc, an enterprising engineer developed a way to apply the stop-start technology he witnessed in his son's car to the factory production lines. Stop-start technology allows a car engine to switch off during brief stops at, say, traffic lights, and then spring back to life in an instant. Adapting this concept to the production line has resulted in fantastic energy savings. As BAE Systems prides itself on technological innovation, this made a brilliant human-interest story in the company magazine. This is much more effective than empty statements of intent or statistics – people can see someone like them doing something and making a difference.

Similarly, lawyers Muckle LLP ran a story about an employee using shredded paper waste as bedding for her horses. 'Happy Horses and Reused Resources' was the headline. The picture of the employee and her happy horse was much more attractive to employees and external stakeholders than a picture of hands holding a planet.

Integration of messages

In one of my workshops, a manufacturing operative, straight off the factory floor and still wearing his dirty overalls, nailed a vital point:

We've got these stickers on the machines telling us to switch them off. But there's nothing in the standard operating procedures about it. It is hammered into us from day one to follow the SOPs, so, if we're not sure, we ignore the stickers. If you want it to happen, it should be in the SOPs.

If you have clear and established messaging channels, the sustainability message must be integrated into those channels. If it is outside those channels then it will remain on the periphery. So sustainability must be integrated into:

- Standard operating procedures.

- Induction training.

- Leaders' statements.

- Company reports.

- Company publications.

- Intranet/websites.

Questions for you

What message are you trying to communicate?

What are the most effective channels?

How can you integrate the message into key existing channels?

cont.

What language should you avoid? What language should you use instead?

How can you better frame the message?

What killer questions will help you open minds to sustainability?

How can you turn the sustainability message into human interest stories?

CHAPTER 4

Engaging Emotionally

LOOKING AT OUR ELEPHANT/RIDER/PATH culture change model, it is the elephant itself that makes the decisions at the end of the day. We like to think we are logical, rational beings, but every one of us is heavily swayed by gut instinct, personal values, irrational prejudices and past experiences both positive and negative. If, say, you want to buy a new car, you would probably analyse performance stats, features and prices and compare them with your needs and budget, but it is often the model you would like to be seen behind the wheel of that you end up choosing. It is this that makes us like Captain Kirk, not Mr Spock.

So how do you engage with the elephant and bring it around to your way of thinking? This is the core of the Green Jujitsu approach – how to tap emotionally into the employee's mind to change their behaviour.

Lead by example

It is very difficult to effect a positive culture change if the organisation's leadership is not on board. Good leadership inspires us and our inner elephants, makes us feel good about the work we do; bad leadership makes us cynical and resentful.

The greatest green business leader is undoubtedly the late Ray Anderson of modular flooring giant InterfaceFLOR. In 1996 he read a book called

The Ecology of Commerce that hit him 'like a spear in the chest'. He swiftly launched a programme called Mission Zero, the objective of which was to have a zero ecological footprint by 2020[7]. To his dying day in 2011, he relentlessly pursued this goal and made quite extraordinary achievements which have proved that business and sustainability were not incompatible.

Another great example is Sir Stuart Rose when he was Chairman and Chief Executive of British retail legend Marks & Spencer. The story goes that Rose saw a screening of Al Gore's documentary film *An Inconvenient Truth* and decided he must act on moral grounds. Insiders say that, as well as this desire to 'do the right thing', Rose was always highly conscious of Marks & Spencer's position as the most trusted brand on the high street and realised that sustainability was a key plank of trust in the 21st century. He made his commitment clear by setting up the Plan A sustainability programme ('because there is no Plan B') and funding it to the tune of £200 million[2].

There are two parts of such inspiring leadership – words and actions – and the two must match. In terms of words, a clear commitment must be made above and beyond the platitudes that most organisations pump out. Ray Anderson rarely spoke in public about anything other than corporate responsibility issues.

These words must be followed by actions, such as Rose's financial commitment. Consistency is a key factor in determining trust, so all business decisions must be as consistent as possible with the green commitment. Where this can't be done, decisions must be explained fully and, where feasible, 'offset' by a new environmental project.

Personal actions can help reinforce the idea that this commitment is not just skin-deep. Leaders can adopt green behaviour in their personal life by, for example, cycling to work, installing solar panels at home, or leading a group of volunteers to dig a pond. Mistakes that can damage personal reputation range from leaving lights on to turning up in a gas-guzzling company car.

The fallback plan: Guerrilla tactics

If you can't get such high-level buy-in for sustainability, all is not lost – you can launch an underground programme and build momentum until it is irresistible. There are myriad examples in history of where small, determined and resourceful bands of fighters have kept much more powerful armies at bay. Again, the Green Jujitsu principle applies – guerrillas who confront their opponents on a conventional battlefield will be annihilated.

The standard guerrilla approach is to get a team of enthusiasts together, then use Green Jujitsu techniques to build up enough projects to demonstrate to the leadership that sustainability is in the interest of the organisation. The use of Green Jujitsu language and questions that we saw in Chapter 3 will be vital weapons on this mission.

Tapping into company culture

Many organisations have a very strong formalised company culture. For example, Canon has a philosophy called '*kyosei*' which translates as 'living and working together for the common good'. The company has subsumed sustainability into *kyosei* culture, a nice piece of Green Jujitsu.

Cultural norms can be less explicit than such a formal philosophy. The example of the standard operating procedures (SOPs) in the last chapter demonstrates this well. The culture in this company, where many of the materials are highly hazardous, was 'follow the SOPs' – if something isn't in the SOPs it is not part of company culture for manufacturing operatives. By embedding sustainability instructions into the SOPs, the company is working with the culture, not against it as it was with the contradictory switch it off labels.

Creating a brand new sustainability centre of gravity such as Marks and Spencer's Plan A is more difficult and risky. It is noticeable that Marks & Spencer is careful to blend Plan A into the mainstream. For example, Plan A communications use the same 'famous faces' as it uses in all its other advertising, creating a seamless continuum between the two. This sends a message to stakeholders inside and outside the company that sustainability is mainstream.

Building trust

Probably the most important factor in working with the elephant is trust. Our inner elephants are often cynical and suspicious, so trust is hard to win and easy to lose. Many of us will have been asked to take part in an exercise where the residual feeling was that we had been used simply to tick a box somewhere to say employees have been consulted and the key decisions had already been made. This kind of breach of trust – 'we want you to have your say, then we'll ignore it' – can completely undermine very hard won progress.

Leadership guru Warren Bennis[8] lists the most important factors influencing our trust as:

1. Competence: the technical and managerial competence to engage properly and deliver on promises.

2. Constancy: the degree to which the organisation/individual can be relied upon to do what it says it will do, even when the going gets tough.

3. Caring: that their welfare is of genuine concern to the organisation/individual.

4. Candour: openness, transparency and honesty, which we will discuss further below.

5. Congruity (or authenticity): that the individual is genuinely committed to what they say they want to do.

These five elements must be embedded into every aspect of the culture change programme. If your employees trust you then your job will be substantially easier.

Show, don't tell

In May 1997, I stood by a roadside in Arctic Russia and looked around at 360° of ecological destruction as far as my eyes could see. On the horizon, chimneys from a nickel smelter pumped sulphurous steam into the sky above me, which would fall as acid rain and scorch the land even more. That day I made a decision – I would dedicate my life to tackling man's impact on the planet. In 2010, *Daily Mail* Science Editor Michael Hanlon went on a trip to Greenland. Before this visit he had been sceptical about climate change, but when he saw the scale of the melt, he changed his mind[9].

Both of these Damascene moments were, strictly speaking, irrational. Before my Arctic experience, I had been an armchair environmentalist and accepted all the science of climate change and acidification. Hanlon had looked at the same information and distrusted it. What each of us witnessed was a tiny part of the world on a single day. I could have been looking at the only acid rain damage in the world and Hanlon could have simply seen normal seasonal ice melt. But that didn't matter. What we felt did. If you witness something with your own eyes, it is the most powerful persuader in the world.

While dragging your entire workforce off to see a glacier melt is beyond the scope of most organisations, you can use similar experiences to get your message across. If you want people to understand how much waste you produce, try piling it up in the car park or factory yard so they can see it for themselves. If you want to demonstrate energy losses then feeling the heat on your face is more powerful than a bar chart on a Powerpoint presentation.

Another option is to get employees involved in hands-on conservation projects. Digging ponds, planting trees and litter picking may be small scale on the grand scale of global environmental pressures, but they do give an experiential, kinaesthetic link between small-scale actions and the planet.

The next best thing to experiencing something yourself is hearing 'someone like you' talking about their experience of that thing. This is why the storytelling approach we looked at in the last chapter is so powerful.

'More stilettos than sandals'

The green movement has a well-earned reputation for presenting sustainability as the hair-shirt option. We are bombarded with litanies of how we should be ashamed of ourselves as a species, often by people who seem to be enjoying lecturing us. There may be some truth in what they say, but how they say it is a turn-off. Hands up who wants a guilt trip?

The answer is to make it fun: ditch the hair-shirt and make sustainability sexy. The 'more stilettos than sandals' maxim came from Ashley Lodge of Harper Collins[10] and it neatly sums up the idea of making sustainability attractive, positive and compelling, not a knotty issue of conscience. I mentioned before those annoying 'Please think about the environment and do not print this email' messages people add to their email signature block. Well, some creative and witty types have rewritten these to put a smile on the reader's face, for example 'Printing this email will make Al Gore cry'[11].

A particularly successful approach to making sustainability fun is to run competitions. Everyone loves a competition and it is very difficult to resist taking part. Lawyers Muckle LLP kicked off their environmental awareness campaign with a multiple choice quiz where employees have to guess the answers to questions such as 'how much paper does the company use per partner per month?' Employees were so shocked by the answer they went on to cut this by two-thirds. Muckle took this further to set an annual competition between the three floors of their offices to see who could best reduce carbon emissions. This approach has also been adopted by drinks giant Diageo, who run a competition between their sites around the globe. Taking part is mandatory and Gold, Silver and Bronze awards are given out to the best performers.

Make people part of the solution

Many staff engagement and culture change programmes see employees as part of the problem. They are not behaving as they should, therefore their behaviour must corrected – like naughty schoolchildren. This adversarial mindset does nothing to inspire the elephant and is the complete antithesis of the Green Jujitsu approach.

My favourite culture change technique is to flip this around and make employees part of the solution by getting them to generate ideas to help the programme. The strengths of this approach are:

- People feel they are being taken seriously.

- Individuals find it difficult to switch off in exercises – so you get more attention.

- You get automatic buy-in as people get excited about their ideas.

- You usually get some excellent new suggestions and will identify barriers to green behaviour.

- If and when those suggestions are implemented then they are more likely to be accepted by employees.

Anyone who has been on one of my training courses will almost certainly have been asked to apply the theory to their organisation. This approach empowers the employees, gives them a deeper understanding of the issues, creates buy-in and gives you a great source of ideas to boot. Annex A describes how I go about this in practice.

Incentives

I was in the middle of a series of assignments for a client with sites across the UK. I knew they were about to hit their annual energy saving target, but I didn't know they had given every employee gift vouchers as a reward. The difference between the sessions before and after the reward was palpable. Everyone was suddenly very interested in energy-saving. 'I feel really guilty – I didn't do anything to contribute to this', one woman told me. 'I suppose I'd better start!'

Incentives are very powerful if done properly, but they can be destructive if done badly. The last thing you want is individuals gaming the system to maximise reward while passing the problem onto others. A great example I have come across is a management consultancy who ran a paper saving competition between their teams. Whoever saved the most paper was able to donate their savings to the charity of their choice. This is very clever – it engaged the teams to act towards a virtuous end.

Teams and teamwork

What can a single designer do to change the lifecycle environmental performance of a complex product, say, a car? If they're really clever (or very lucky) that individual might come up with some revolutionary new aerodynamic tweak which leads to a huge improvement in fuel efficiency, but it is very unlikely. On the other hand, if the whole product development team is tasked with greening the vehicle, that's a different matter – they can determine the overall design concept, optimise every component and subsystems and exploit synergies between innovations.

Elephants are herd animals and prefer to move in groups. In the same way, we can use teams as an intermediary between the individual and the corporation as a whole. This has many opportunities:

- Empowerment: working together, the team has the power to actually change things.

- Purpose: at the team level, the relevance of sustainability to the job role is very tangible.

- Camaraderie: the team has a common mission and will help each other achieve it.

- Peer pressure: loyalty to fellow team members is often stronger than loyalty to the organisation overall.

While these are advantages, they can initially be barriers – sometimes it is hard to win over the trust of a tightly knit team and individual members can sometimes hide behind formal or informal leaders to avoid having to change. The best approach to overcome this is of course Green Jujitsu – working to strengths rather than weaknesses, for example:

- Tailor all sustainability communications to the team's role.

- Illustrate awareness material with case studies of team effort.

- Challenge the team to come up with sustainability solutions for their role.

- Give the team leader personal responsibility to deliver sustainability goals.

- Aim incentives and rewards at the team as a whole.

Questions for you

Are your leaders committed to sustainability?

If not, how can you use the techniques in Chapters 3 and 4 to get their commitment?

What positive aspects of company culture can you tap into?

How can you use 'show, don't tell' experiences to engage staff members?

Are your sustainability communications and programmes engaging and fun?

How can you utilise competitions and incentives to engage staff members?

Can you make your employees part of the solution?

How can you utilise teams within the organisation to maximise the effectiveness of your engagement?

CHAPTER 5

Nudging People Onto The Right Path

PEOPLE (AND ELEPHANTS) TEND to take the path of least resistance to any goal. You only have to look at how people cut corners when walking along actual paths to create short cuts. While this is often seen as a problem, it can be harnessed to your advantage, shaping the path to encourage elephants to go where you'd like them to. The book *Nudge* popularised the idea of altering behaviour by making 'bad' behaviour difficult and 'good' behaviour easy by altering the 'architecture' of choices[12].

So to encourage sustainable behaviour you must make good behaviour easy (e.g. promote cycling to work by providing good quality, covered cycle racks plus showers and lockers) and 'bad' behaviour should be more difficult (e.g. charging for staff parking permits). This section looks at various options for embedding this kind of thinking into your organisation.

Providing green technology

An obvious pre-requisite of green behaviour is having the infrastructure available to allow that behaviour. This is analogous to the elephant having an alternative path in the first place – many organisations seem to expect individuals to make their own. Examples include:

- Teleconferencing facilities to eliminate unnecessary business travel.

- Telecommuting facilities along with policies to promote working from home.

- Low carbon vehicles.

- Water efficient facilities such as multi-flush toilets.

- Zoned heating and lighting to match work patterns so only the minimum needs to be switched on in any circumstances.

- Recycling facilities.

Of course, once you have provided the technology you have to use the other Green Jujitsu techniques to ensure that they are actually used.

You can take this a step further forward and use automation to take individuals out of the loop altogether. Automatic lighting, heating/ventilation controls and IT systems (e.g. 'Nightwatchman' software) can all save energy in this way.

Changing the physical environment

When I first got started in this career, I routinely used to suggest to clients that if they really wanted to boost paper recycling in their offices they should take away everyone's general waste bins and give them a paper recycling bin. A general waste bin could be put in the corner of the office or at the end of the corridor – reversing standard practice where if people wanted to recycle, they had to trek to the recycling bin. In most cases those clients looked at me as if I were mad. Now this shift in bins is fast becoming standard practice.

This is a classic example of a nudge – rearranging the physical work environment to make green behaviour easier and 'bad' behaviour harder. Other examples include:

- Put cycle parking next to the front entrance, not at the far end of the car park.

- Likewise, place electric vehicle charging bays closer to the front door than other pool vehicles.

- Make it difficult to light an entire building with one switch, but easy to switch off lights all at once.

- Place staircases as a shorter and more obvious route than lifts in low rise buildings.

Policy changes

A 'perverse incentive' is policy which encourages people to do the 'wrong' thing. These must be hunted down and eliminated with extreme prejudice. In a recent engagement session I conducted at a major international company, someone complained that no-one was using the company's teleconferencing system. When we explored why not, we discovered that in order to calculate the financial benefits of the system the company made it a condition of booking that an estimation of avoided staff travel time and travel costs had to be provided. So you'd have to sit down and work out where everyone was coming from, how they were travelling, how long it would take them, what each person's hourly cost was and what fares/hire car charges/mileage they would incur. And then add it all up and then you could use the system. Most people are unfamiliar with teleconferencing, so by putting this extra burden on 'good' behaviour, staff were just sticking to the same old 'bad' behaviour they were used to – booking a conference room and letting everyone make their own travel arrangements. You can hardly blame them.

Where perverse incentives are found, they need to be flipped around to nudge people towards sustainable behaviour. Another client of mine changed their travel booking policy so that booking a train fare was done in house for you, but if you wanted a short-haul flight, you had to book and pay for it yourself and claim back the cost. So while you still had the choice, it was much more of a hassle to fly.

Other policy opportunities include:

- Removing higher mileage rates for larger cars.

- Incentivising the purchase of low carbon vehicles for company cars.

- Implementing a mileage rate for cycling.

- Adding extra checks and balances to the purchase of hazardous materials, while providing lists of non-hazardous alternatives.

Identifying problems and opportunities

The best way to identify opportunities to shape the working environment to foster good behaviour is to ask your employees. Why do they follow certain paths? What would help them change? Front-line staff in particular often have a completely different view of how a company operates (some would say they know how it really operates).

This process can be combined with 'making people part of the solution' covered in Chapter 4. In fact, when I do staff engagement sessions with clients, I always offer the option of capturing ideas generated and feeding them back into the clients' business improvement processes. This has the added benefit of demonstrating that the solutions generation sessions are meaningful as participants can see their ideas being taken seriously.

Questions for you

Which green technologies would give your employees the opportunity to pursue greener behaviour?

How can you alter the physical layout of your working environment to promote green behaviour?

How can you alter bureaucratic processes and policies to promote green behaviour?

What perverse incentives will need to be flipped around?

How can you get the right insight into working life to identify these opportunities?

CHAPTER 6

Human Resources Issues

WHILE THE GREEN JUJITSU APPROACH is very powerful for culture change, it will work best within a human resources (HR) structure designed to promote sustainability. In this chapter we will consider some of the supporting functions which can be altered to maximise its effectiveness. As we will see, there are also opportunities to embed the Green Jujitsu approach into that HR structure.

Recruitment

It is a truism that organisations are groups of people rather than entities in their own right. If you want a particular culture, then recruiting people whose attitudes are compatible with sustainability makes a good foundation for your efforts. However, I have found that it is generally easier to teach a good engineer about sustainability than it is to teach an environmental expert about engineering.

The good news is that companies with a good reputation on environmental and ethical issues have been shown to attract more applicants, so you will have more to choose from, which makes it more likely that you will find candidates who are great at their job and interested in sustainability.

To maximise this opportunity, sustainability issues should be incorporated into the whole recruitment process. Examples include:

- Pre-application information, for example, the 'Working at ACME plc' section of the website.

- Application briefing and job description (see below).

- Questions on application forms and interview process.

- Content of orientation tours, etc.

This will warm up new recruits so they arrive with an idea of the company culture they will be working in.

Job descriptions and performance assessment

One of the biggest mistakes an organisation can make is to have a misalignment between responsibility and authority when it comes to sustainability. If you want to give someone responsibility for a particular aspect of sustainability, then they must have the authority to act. Traditionally, environmental managers have had huge amounts of responsibility (including keeping their bosses out of jail) but precious little authority.

Clearly, the most effective way to fix this disconnect is to give specific sustainability responsibilities to those who already have sufficient authority to act – people such as site managers, production managers and heads of procurement. This integration of sustainability into core jobs is a leap away from the traditional environmental manager beavering away fruitlessly in his or her green silo.

It follows that if you give someone responsibility and authority, you must also give them accountability. So the responsibility must be backed up with targets which should be reviewed in performance assessment. This is particularly important for middle management who tend to be very target oriented.

Formal training

Training sessions are a great opportunity to promote environmental sustainability to individuals. Green Jujitsu techniques can be incorporated into training itself:

- Incorporating sustainability into as many 'mainstream' training courses as possible, particularly induction training, so it is seen to be part of the mainstream and not a fringe topic.

- Tailor sustainability training to job roles to make it as relevant as possible to individuals' daily routine.

- Use storytelling in case studies to show how sustainability is driven by 'people like us'.

- Use exercises to get participants to generate sustainability solutions to drive relevance and buy-in to the process.

Who does the changing?

One of the biggest questions is whether to form a sustainability team or not, and how that team should be constituted. There are four main options, all but the last can be mixed and matched:

- Formal, dedicated sustainability staff team.

- Part-time staff committee: volunteer members who have 'day jobs' but meet periodically to review and monitor progress.

- Part-time sustainability, green or energy 'champions' who are asked to encourage sustainability in their immediate working environment.

- No team: either use a facilitator to work with staff across business functions or the 'benign dictatorship' approach of small companies with strong and determined leaders.

The advantages of the four systems are given in Table 2.

TABLE 2: Advantages of different staffing approaches.

Dedicated team	Part-time committee	Sustainability champions	No team
Ensures required expertise in house	Cross-section of functions represented	Cross-section of functions represented	Ownership with mainstream employees
Defined responsibility and accountability	Buy-in ensured Centre of gravity around which activity can take place	Cheaper than formal team – only part-time requirement of staff time	No 'us and them' ghettoisation of 'green'
More projects can be launched and monitored	Much cheaper than formal team in terms of salaries	Local 'experts' can apply their domain knowledge	Agile – no bureaucracy Cheap – no bureaucracy
Less chance of issues 'falling between stools'	Can be effective in a 'leadership vacuum'	Peer-to-peer communications may be better trusted	

Different companies use different combinations of these approaches depending on their company culture. Whichever approach is adopted, it is important that the individuals are trained in the Green Jujitsu approach. One approach that is widely misused, in my opinion, is the use of 'champions', so we will look at that in more detail.

Sustainability/environmental champions

One of the most common first steps large organisations make in sustainability programmes is to appoint sustainability champions throughout the functions and ranks. The usual argument for doing so is that champions are embedded into the organisation and can provide peer-to-peer support to other staff members who want change their behaviour and act as local flag-wavers for corporate green goals.

This is great in theory, but peer-to-peer by definition is bottom-up, appointing people to roles is top-down and I believe that is a fundamental conflict. I've also seen the champion role seriously abused. I've seen junior volunteers given energy efficiency targets for entire sites, I've seen them (post-volunteering) being expected to read energy meters on a regular basis, and I've heard of them being expected to get into work before everyone else to check who has switched their computers off. As a result of this lack of definition, many champion programmes descend into forums for complaint.

So what's the alternative? Well, if you want to engage with green thinking people, why not create a club to glean their ideas and share what is happening in the organisation? Then the peer-to-peer communication will come out organically rather than the artificial champion version.

The other option is to appoint green champions, but give them a well-defined role and training in Green Jujitsu-style behavioural change. Involve them in company-wide engagement programmes as facilitators and solutions generators, but don't expect them to work miracles on your behalf.

External change agents

There are advantages in employing an external change agent such as a consultant to engage with employees:

- A lack of baggage: external people do not bring with them the toxic effects of office politics, prejudices or bad blood that internal change agents may be saddled with.

- External agents generally come with a breadth of experience from working with a wide range of organisations which can help provoke or stimulate new thinking.

- Culture change is difficult and specialist skills are required to get the programme off on the right foot.

The disadvantages of using an external agent are:

- It can be difficult to walk onto someone else's patch and persuade them to change what they are doing without getting a negative reaction. However, there are tools and techniques to overcome this (see Annex A).

- It can be difficult to hand over to permanent staff without loss of momentum, but long-term ownership must reside within the organisation.

Questions for you

Does your recruitment process get the right message over to potential recruits?

Is responsibility aligned to authority and vice versa in your organisation?

Do you incorporate sustainability into 'mainstream' training, for example, induction courses?

Does your formal sustainability training utilise Green Jujitsu techniques?

Do your change agents have the necessary Green Jujitsu skills and experiences?

Could an external change agent help?

Conclusions

CULTURE CHANGE IS WIDELY REGARDED as the single biggest challenge for organisations wishing to embrace sustainability. The standard response to this challenge is often primitive – switch it off stickers, awareness posters and clichéd proclamations from the great and the good – and ultimately ineffective.

The Green Jujitsu approach presented in this e-book is incredibly powerful, but subtle. It is all about understanding your audience, gauging their strengths and interests, and tailoring your programme to exploit those strengths and interests. While this may appear on the face of it to be obvious, it is worth noting that most sustainability culture change programmes take the exact opposite approach.

We have covered a whole toolbox of Green Jujitsu techniques within the elephant/rider/path model of culture change:

- The rider: tailoring the message to the rider, rather than expecting the rider to become 'converted'.

- The elephant: engaging on a deeper emotional level by truly involving individuals in the process.

- The path: altering the working environment and rules to encourage green behaviour and discourage ungreen behaviour.

My favoured technique across all three aspects of the elephant model is to involve all employees in solutions generation. This can identify

CONCLUSIONS

problems and opportunities in informing the rider and shaping the path, all the while inspiring the elephant.

So, once you start implementing the Green Jujitsu approach, how do you know if your efforts are working? You should look out for the following telltale signs:

- People look pleased to see you.

- Colleagues start knocking on your door to ask your advice.

- Colleagues start knocking on your door with new suggestions.

- Your key performance indicators start improving faster than you expected.

- The boss takes a genuine interest.

- Spontaneous projects start springing up all over your organisation and you struggle to keep up with them.

- Other people start trying to muscle in and/or take credit.

- Your staff start bragging about the company's achievements.

- New recruits tell you that the organisation's green efforts attracted them to the business.

To start seeing these signs of progress takes a lot of work – working harder and smarter. The Green Jujitsu approach requires a certain amount of humility, a huge amount of astuteness and, above all, an infinite supply of perseverance. Whatever you do, however hard it can seem at times, keep going, keep trying stuff, keep thinking and keep doing what works.

....

ANNEX

Group Exercises

Overview

THIS ANNEX GIVES SOME INSIGHT into how I run group engagement sessions. Clearly, different people will want to adapt this to maximise their own strengths and circumstances, but this is the way I maximise the benefits of the Green Jujitsu approach.

Powerpoint or not?

A wag once said 'all power corrupts, but PowerPoint corrupts absolutely'. While I often use this useful technology to illustrate my talks and to back up my longer training sessions, I am increasingly trying to eradicate PowerPoint from my shorter stakeholder engagement sessions whether for employees or external people. I have run many sessions with up to 40 delegates with just a flipchart, a marker pen, a selection of Post-Its and some A0 prints of my brainstorming tools.

The problems with using PowerPoint are:

- Audiences are now indoctrinated with the idea that once the screen goes up they can sit back in their chair and go into passive listening mode or go into critic mode.

- It can be difficult to switch between 'presentation mode' and 'interactive mode'.

- PowerPoint can be horribly misused with reams of bullet point laden slides.

Setting PowerPoint aside can make for a refreshing change.

Gaining immediate buy-in

My standard opening for an engagement session is to stand beside a blank flipchart sheet and ask 'Why are we here?' I quickly explain that I don't mean in a metaphysical sense, but why is the organisation interested in sustainability (or whatever subset of sustainability we are working with).

There are a number of reasons for starting like this:

- You throw the delegates straight into the issue, before they have time to sit back and cross their arms.

- They sell the business case for sustainability (and the need for the session) to themselves and each other, rather than you having to try to persuade them.

- You get a flavour of the thinking of the delegates so you can tweak the tone and content of the rest of the session to match.

I write their responses up on a flip chart and keep asking them for more until they've got all the most important ones. The knack is not to be afraid of silence – ask 'anything else' and wait, marker poised until someone speaks up. Once we have finished, I leave the flipchart up as it is often useful to refer back to it later on in the session.

Solutions generation

The process revolves around the Terra Infirma Brainstorming tool (see Figure 3). This has been designed to give some structure to brainstorming without throttling the conversation. It basically gives four generic ways of contributing to an environmental goal at the head of the fishbone diagram. The top two are about doing the right thing, the bottom two about doing things right. The left-hand two are about people and the right-hand two are about hardware. So the four are:

- Procedures (people doing the right thing): are the official procedures designed to allow and encourage the desired behaviour of staff members (or others)? Do they discourage or bar undesired behaviour? How would they need to change?

- Behaviour (people doing things right): are people actually behaving in the right way? What training might they need? What techniques from Chapters 4 and 5 would encourage them to behave differently?

- Technology (the right hardware): do you have the right equipment, software and/or materials? What would make a positive difference?

- Application (hardware being applied correctly): has that technology been installed and set up correctly? Is it being maintained properly? (The actual operation of the equipment would come under Procedures and Behaviour.)

Just to take the example of a compressed air system:

- If the compressor itself needs upgrading, that solution would come under Technology.

- If the airlines are not being checked for leaks, the solutions would come under Application.

- If the compressed air is being misused such as squirting fellow employees, then a formal rule banning this would come under Procedures.

- Behaviour solutions could include providing feedback on the amount of compressed air being used and how much it costs.

Here's how I will typically use the tool:

- Customise a version of the tool for each of your organisations' sustainability targets by writing the target in the 'head' of the fishbone (e.g. Carbon Neutral, Zero Waste).

- Print one copy of each version on an A0 sheet and stick the sheets around the walls of the training room.

- Split the delegates into teams of at least three per team, introduce the tool and assign a team to each sheet.

- Give each team a different colour of Post-It notes and challenge them to think of solutions, write each one on a Post-It and stick it to the appropriate part of the brainstorming tool.

- After 8–15 minutes, rotate the teams so each has a different sheet. Using the same colour of Post-It as they had before, challenge them to think of solutions that the previous team(s) hadn't thought of.

- Continue rotating the teams until every team has had a go at each sheet which should now be covered in a rainbow of Post-Its.

- Challenge the teams to pick the best three solutions they have thought of across the different sheets.

The AO sheets are highly effective. They are fresh and novel for most participants, a big group can crowd around them, they encourage a more kinaesthetic approach to the problem, and the big sheet takes a lot of filling with Post-Its, encouraging more ideas. The rotation means that the exercise gets more and more difficult as time goes on, making teams think harder and keeping their attention.

....

FIGURE 3. Terra Infirma Brainstorming tool.

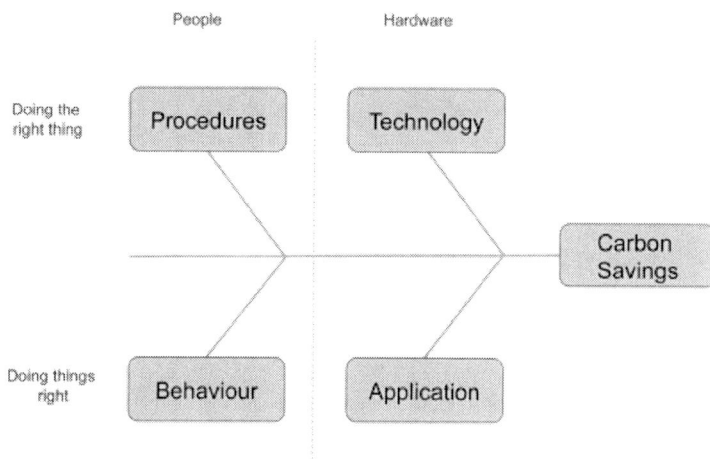

People   Hardware

Doing the right thing — Procedures   Technology

Carbon Savings

Doing things right — Behaviour   Application

....

References

1. Amory Lovins, Rocky Mountain Institute, speaking at Schumacher College, Devon, 2002.

2. Kane, G. 2011. *The Green Executive: Corporate Leadership for a Low Carbon Economy* (London: Earthscan).

3. Figure adapted from Thompson, M., Ellis, R. and Widavsky, A. 1990. *Cultural Theory* (Boulder, CO: Westview Press).

4. Heath, C. and Heath, D. 2010. *Switch: How to Change Things When Change is Hard* (New York: Random House Business).

5. For more on this, see Senge, P.M., Smith, B., Schley, S., Laur, J. and Kruschwitz, N. 2008. *The Necessary Revolution: How Individuals and Organizations are Working Together to Create a Sustainable World* (London: Nicholas Brearley Publishing).

6. See http://www.energysavingtrust.org.uk/In-your-home/Your-energy-supply/Smart-meters.

7. Anderson, R. 2010. *Confessions of a Radical Industrialist: How Interface Proved That You Can Build a Successful Business without Destroying the Planet* (London: Random House Business).

8. Bennis, W. 1999. The leadership advantage. *Leader To Leader* (No. 12, Spring), http://www.leadertoleader.org/knowledgecenter/journal.aspx?ArticleID=53.

9. See   http://www.dailymail.co.uk/sciencetech/article-1301713/The-crack-roof-world-Yes-global-warming-real--deeply-worrying.html.

10. Ashley Lodge, Harper Collins, speaking at the Low Carbon Innovation Exchange, London, 26 June 2008.

REFERENCES

11. See   http://www.deliverfreedom.com/blog/offices-going-green-funny-email-taglines/.

12. Thaler, R.H. and Sunstein, C.R. 2008. *Nudge: Improving Decisions about Health, Wealth and Happiness* (London: Penguin).

....

How Gamification Can Help Your Business Engage in Sustainability

Paula Owen

paula@paulaowenconsulting.co.uk

www. paulaowenconsulting.co.uk

www.ecoactiongames.org.uk

Abstract

A NEW, INNOVATIVE ENGAGEMENT theory has been quietly permeating the business world over recent years, and it answers to the name of 'gamification'. In a relatively short time, the ideas and thinking behind gamification have begun to circulate through the corporate community and beyond, and are now causing widening ripples of interest in other more diverse sectors of society. The term, virtually unknown just a few years ago, is now being widely discussed, and its concepts implemented, in sectors as diverse as health and fitness,[1] medical research,[2] the financial sector[3] and through to even achieving the seemingly impossible task of making mundane domestic chores[4] exciting. Its relatively early accomplishments in these areas throw up an intriguing question for sustainability professionals: 'If it works successfully in these sectors, what might be its potential for encouraging pro-environmental engagement and behaviour change in the environmental sector?' The main goals of gamification are increased user interaction, behavioural change and the stimulation of innovative thinking and the generation of new ideas. But what is gamification in practice? Is it simply the latest 'flash-in-the-pan' techie-led fad? Does it actually have the substance required to establish itself as a genuinely useful business tool for deepening and strengthening engagement? Moreover, and more importantly for organisations concerned with enhancing their environmental sustainability, can it be developed and implemented in such a way as to help persuade customers, employees, shareholders, executives and board members

ABSTRACT

alike to become more sustainable in their purchasing habits, everyday working lives and investment choices? This DōShort investigates and reports on the current state of play (no pun intended), thinking and theories concerning gamification, and its potential role in deepening the level of engagement in the sustainability agenda, in this its early stage of evolution. It draws together the emerging facts, examples of early adopters and existing practice to help businesses decide whether the tools of gamification can be applied in engaging their own customers, staff and other stakeholders in more sustainable practices.

....

About the Author

PAULA OWEN has worked in sustainability for over two decades. She began her career in academia, gaining a PhD in climate change chemistry from Oxford University. However, she quickly realised she couldn't spend her entire life in darkened laboratories and so changed tack slightly to concentrate on the communicating of environmental and scientific concepts and issues to general audiences.

Since then she has worked for environmental charities, within in the public sector, through secondments in central government, and in 2010 she set up her own research, authorship, training and advice agency focusing on environmental sustainability generally, and energy and carbon management in particular. She relishes the challenges of working with a diverse selection of clients from blue chip companies, environmental charities, through arts and funding bodies to international NGOs.

She is a published author and has written widely on the subject of energy efficiency within the domestic sector. She was the project manager for the award-winning UK Government's Act on CO_2 carbon calculator.

Over the past years she has become more convinced that behaviour change and engaging the majority is vital if we are to make progress environmentally. In 2012 she was awarded a London Leaders position by the London Sustainable Development Commission, and Unltd Social Entrepreneur award funding, to further her work in researching the power of fun and games to help save the planet.

....

Acknowledgments

I WOULD LIKE TO THANK Nicoletta Landi for her help as both a researcher on the case studies used in this book and for her skill at proof-reading and language checking and Jamie Beevor for passing his reliably analytical eye over my more fanciful ideas and flowery prose and keeping me in check.

CHAPTER 1

Introducing Gamification: A Flash in the Pan or the Next Big Thing?

A short history of gamification

IN 2005, A US-BASED START-UP company began exploring the potential of using the established theories of social games and games mechanics, taking and translating the concepts and applying them to non-game situations and sectors. This novel approach was seen to work successfully in a variety of contexts over the following years and, consequently, a new business engagement concept was born. That company was called Bunchball[5] and its founder, Rajat Paharia, coined the term 'gamification' for the first time around the year 2010 to give the concept an identity.

In just a few years, the broad concept, theories and practices of gamification have taken off in a diverse range of sectors. The business world has begun to embrace the idea to help it find new and compelling ways to engage with its customers, its staff and other stakeholders. Gamification advocates claim it offers the potential for businesses to gain competitive advantage, deepen relationships with customers and retain their custom for longer. From the employee engagement perspective it is claimed to help improve productivity, increase staff morale and lead to an increasingly engaged, more hard-working and switched-on workforce.

INTRODUCING GAMIFICATION:
A FLASH IN THE PAN OR THE NEXT BIG THING?

By utilising similar principles that make both traditional games and online social media games appealing and compelling, i.e. encapsulating a sense of fun, competition, achievement, gratification, improvement and rewards, businesses are beginning to take notice of its potential. In particular, they are looking to gamification to increase that holy triumvirate of staff productivity, customer loyalty and, of course, bottom-line profitability. Crucially, it also provides an alternative way in to reach out to a younger sector of consumers, customers, clients and potential employees: basically the strata of society born around and after 1990, brought up in a wholly digital age and nicknamed 'Generation Y' or the 'digital natives', those who have never known a pre-Internet world. This sector of society is often somewhat impervious to the traditional methods of communication and advertising and requires something much more interactive, novel and challenging to engage their attention in any meaningful and long-lasting way.

Finding a single dictionary definition of gamification that is universally adopted is difficult. The gamification wiki,[6] probably the largest compendium of information on the subject, offers the following definition:

> Gamification is the concept of applying game-design thinking to non-game applications to make them more fun and engaging. Gamification can potentially be applied to any industry and almost anything to create fun and engaging experiences, converting *users* into *players*.

The idea of turning 'users', a relatively reactive term, into 'players', a term that suggests proactive engagement, effort and activity, is a key element of the gamification process. The notion of evolving passive consumers or employees from simply recipients of products/services or commands/

orders respectively into active, engaged, enthusiastic proponents of whatever the organisation is 'selling' is a powerful driver for businesses. To convert both customers and staff into positive and vocal advocates for the brand has a strong pull and, indeed, marketers have been using this approach for some time. This is why, in these early days of the evolution of gamification, businesses are beginning to prick up their ears and take note of the early successes in this area.

Indeed, a Gartner report[7] released in 2011, predicted that by 2015 more than 50% of organisations that are involved in innovation processes would be 'gamifying' those processes, and, it reported, in a matter of just a few years the ideas of gamification, for consumer marketing and customer retention, would be just as important as those behemoths of twenty-first century engagement and commerce: Facebook, eBay and Amazon. The main goals of gamification, according to Gartner, are increased user interaction, behavioural change, the stimulation of innovative thinking and the generation of new ideas. Wouldn't that be a breath of fresh air in the increasingly rather stale world of employee engagement initiatives and other environmental improvement programmes?

Deloitte, in their Tech Trends report,[8] devote a whole chapter to the topic, and have come up with their own snappy definition: 'gamification is about taking the essence of games – fun, play, passion – and applying it to real-world, non-game situations'. They cite it as one of their Top Ten trends to watch over the coming years and highlighting 2012 as the year that 'gamification moves beyond entertainment to business performance, using intuitive design, intrinsic motivation and the sense of accomplishment that comes from completing activities with clear and personal values'.

Deloitte goes on to say: 'In a business setting, that means designing solutions using gaming principles in everything from back-office tasks to training to sales management and career counselling.'

The very idea of games, online gaming and 'gamers' being at the heart of the development of any seriously debated, potentially important business tool might seem anathema to some. Anyone who feels that computer or other 'online' games, particularly of the 'shoot 'em up' variety, are just a colossal waste of time may have a particularly hard time swallowing the potential of gamification as an effective business engagement technique. However, what is becoming increasingly apparent is, by exploring the pared-down principles of good games design and applying the fundamentals of game mechanics to existing processes, there appears to be a tremendous amount of potential for the business community.

The gender-based argument that any type of 'gaming' focused solution, business related or otherwise, would only appeal to males, and to a certain more youthful age bracket, also seems to not hold water as the average game player today clocks in at a mature 37 years old and over 40% of all game players are female (McGonigal, 2011).

Indeed, already we have seen successful gamified applications in widely diversified areas: for example, in health and fitness,[9] where there is a whole host of online applications, such as myfitnesspal and Fitocracy, that help individuals lose weight and take up more exercise through the use of online score (calories consumed versus calories burnt) keeping, sharing successes with friends in an online community and daily challenges. In medical research[10] we see the phenomenal success of the Foldit project which is discussed in Chapter 2; and on to the financial sector[11] where the online help tool Saveup.com, for example, allows people to more easily manage their money through making financial management into a game. Finally, there is even the 'sexing up' of mundane domestic chores[12] a hitherto seemingly impossible challenge overcome by a simple online game, Chore Wars, which turns completing household tasks into a challenge within household or office environments of who can score the most points, top the leader board and win prizes by completing otherwise shunned and oft-avoided tasks.

The influential US-based Pew Research Center, as part of their 'Pew Internet and American Life project', recently published a report into the future of gamification[13] as predicted by a survey of over one thousand internet experts, tech analysts, critics and stakeholders. In it they concluded that experts 'generally believe the use of game mechanics, feedback loops and rewards will become more embedded in daily life by 2020'.

They went on to predict that the results of such a 'gamification' process could have both positive and negative consequences. On the plus side, they said that the 'move to implement more game elements in networked communications will be mostly positive, aiding education, health, business and training'. However, they also signed a note of caution regarding the potential for 'invisible, insidious behaviour manipulation' through the use of such interventions.

Indeed, already we are seeing reports of the nascent gamification industry being worth $100 million, and that is predicted grow to $2.8 billion by 2016 according to a 2012 forecast[14] by M2 Research, a US-based analysis firm, that is assessing the trends in gamification worldwide.

So what does the idea and implementation of 'gamification' principles within a sustainable business environment entail? Moreover, how can these principles be applied to environmental improvement and engagement in sustainability generally? We discuss these questions next.

What role for gamification in educating for sustainability?

This DōShort argues that gamification has much potential as a new method for engaging people – staff, stakeholders, consumers, customers and clients – in environmental action. But how is it different to what has gone before? Moreover, can it offer new insights into the complex area of motivation, retention and action for sustainability in the longer term? To frame these questions we look back at the world of environmental campaigning and educating over recent decades.

Ever since the emergence of an organised global environmental pressure movement in the early 1970s, through the creation of pressure groups such as Greenpeace, a predominant focus of campaigns to galvanise the public into action has been on the doom and gloom, 'act now or pay later' style of campaigning. For many acute situations and environmental disasters, such as oil spills or deforestation, company malpractices or single issue debates, such as Greenpeace's early focus on 'saving the whale', inciting a sense of injustice, anger and possibly even guilt (i.e. implying that inaction could signify a passive acceptance of the situation) worked effectively in mobilising hundreds of thousands of latent activists across the globe to take action – whether directly or through a more 'armchair activism' approach of monetary donations to the cause.

The 1970s and 1980s, in particular, saw the rise of the amateur environmentalist – ordinary citizens with a passion for the issues and a strong understanding of the original cause of the problem and the ultimate effect that it was having, and how they could help to solve the situation by clear, unambiguous actions. Reasonably clear-cut, 'cause and effect' issues were the typical campaign route. They were typically localised (but not always), and generally had a clearly defined 'enemy' to be thwarted – be it the CFCs in aerosols that were destroying the ozone layer, or the pollution from dirty factories that caused 'acid rain' resulting in lakes and rivers hundreds of miles away becoming poisoned and lifeless. People could take action, whether it be boycotting aerosol cans, tuna from unsustainable companies or products from factories that were causing the pollution; they felt empowered and crucially believed that their actions could and would make a positive difference. The feedback loop also, although not by any means instantaneous, did report that slowly, but steadily, such concerted, individual actions were truly making a difference – the ozone hole was slowly repairing itself, poisoned lakes were coming back to life and fishing companies were changing their unsustainable practices.

Roll on to the early years of the twenty-first century and those clearly identified, reasonably unambiguous environmental nemeses of the past have been more or less superseded by a more obscure, disparate, multi-faceted foe. Issues that used to be neatly defined, pigeon-holed and dealt with through focused, results-driven campaigns now manifest themselves as much more complex, equivocal and harder to pinpoint the cause and effect. They are typically argued about endlessly on the TV, in print media and on the new democratising medium of the World Wide Web.

We are talking, of course, about the environmental issue that has trumped all others in terms of its global significance and long-term potential for disruption – accelerated, anthropogenic climate change. It is with this globally weighty, but messy and indistinct issue that the environmental sector's players – those being the activists, campaigners and communicators – missed a trick when it came to the vital task of informing, educating, inspiring and galvanising the wider public into taking positive, pro-environmental action against climatic change. Despite being a new issue, the methods employed to communicate it remained firmly anchored in the past. Potentially a reflection of an 'if it ain't broke, don't fix it' mentality, the issue under discussion may have changed, but the tone and approach of delivering the message has remained the same. The 'scare them with the bare facts and they are bound to take action' approach worked in the past, so who was to say it wouldn't work this time around?

Consequently, the approach to climate change communications and education has tended to focus on the 'doom and gloom' aspects – which, of course, are understandable: there is a lot to be gloomy about! However, the sheer vastness of the issue, combined with the non-acute, longer-term, probability-based range of potential effects, and continuing debates on the uncertainties of the science, did and do little to inspire ordinary folk into action. Indeed, the opposite effect can occur, with people arguing themselves into inaction as they do not believe that they alone, as individuals, can actually make any impact whatsoever in solving this issue.[15]

Typically, calls to action on climate change related issues have tended to lean towards the 'misery messaging' end of the communication spectrum, with a large dollop of guilt thrown in for good measure. The 'change your ways or the polar bear will die' style of campaigning may work on small children and the 'charismatic mega fauna' enthusiasts amongst us, but is not a message that will inspire sustained, practical action in the masses.

A backward glance at the rather unfortunate film media advertising campaigns of both the UK government's 'Act on CO_2' (a primetime TV advert where a father is reading a bedtime story to his child about how climate change would soon devastate their environment and most famously featuring a drowning puppy[16]) and the campaign group 10:10's ill-conceived, Richard Curtis-penned short film *No Pressure*[17] where children and adults who didn't take carbon-reducing actions were graphically blown up in a range of locations, are a few extreme examples on how badly in the wrong direction the climate change messaging and 'calls to action' have veered over recent years.

In the grand scheme of things, a bad news story, or a guilt-tinged messaging campaign will have some short-term success. It will have an effect on latent, would-be greenies who need that last nudge into taking action. For people who have guilt as a motivator in their lives this approach can also work. However, it is not an approach that alone will enjoy mass appeal and engage the majority to take action in the longer term.

This is where gamification can step into the breach. As, by its very nature, it is a positive, inclusive, action-oriented approach to education, influencing and ultimately behaviour change, it could be a major 'game changer' in the sustainability world. The appeal of games, in their broadest form and manifestations, are their very wide multi-generational draw. Most people, at some point in their lives, have played and been absorbed by a game – from simple single-player cards games such as Patience and Solitaire to that kids' perennial favourite Trumps, to chess,

INTRODUCING GAMIFICATION:
A FLASH IN THE PAN OR THE NEXT BIG THING?

Scrabble, Monopoly, Cluedo and Risk, all the way through to the earliest electronic games such as Tetris, Space Invaders and bringing it up to date with the hugely popular Massive Multiplayer Online (MMOPS) type of game such as World of Warfare.

Games are fun, and unless you are a particularly sore loser, one's experience of playing them is typically rewarding, entertaining, occasionally educational (Trivial Pursuit, Scrabble or trump style games, for example) and generally sociable. Hence the idea of using some of the underlying concepts that make up the theory and practice of games design and mechanics to bring a fresh approach to education and engagement in environmental issues seems, in theory at least, a reasonable starting point for a method of engagement.

Before moving on to discuss the implications of gamification on environmental issues, it must be made clear that this is not advocating the trivialising of an issue as globally disruptive and serious as climate change by attempting to turn it into a game. Instead we are exploring the potential of turning communications, educational initiatives and 'calls to action' pertaining to climate change and other environmental issues, into more positive messages around how such actions can be aspirational and constructive to assist widespread take-up.

To explore some of these ideas we first need to look at the concepts that gamification is based on, namely: the ideas of social games and social media games, game mechanics and game design techniques. We look more closely at these concepts in the next chapter.

....

CHAPTER 2

Elements of the Theory:
The Lego Set of Gamification

ALTHOUGH HAILED AS AN INNOVATIVE, twenty-first-century business tool, gamification has its roots firmly planted in the science and art of game mechanics and design that go back decades if not millennia. The modern idea of using games and gaming techniques as a model for re-defining and re-imagining existing processes is borne from the research and writings of leading online games developers and thought-leaders such as Jane McGonigal, Gabe Zicherman and Jon Radoff (see further reading for references). Interestingly, all three of them have brought out best-selling books exploring various aspects of gamifying real life, business and marketing in the last few years.

McGonigal, in her seminal book *Reality is Broken: Why Games Make Us Better and How They Can Change the World*, provides a strong argument around the power of games as a tool to re-engage people in societal change. In it she argues that modern life, as millions of us live it in the developed world at least, often ceases to provide the interesting, rewarding, absorbing, satisfying hard work that most of us crave – consciously or subconsciously. This is why, she posits, online games, computer-generated worlds and gaming generally have become so tremendously popular in recent decades.

ELEMENTS OF THE THEORY:
THE LEGO SET OF GAMIFICATION

This other virtual, alternative world, where ordinary folk can become heroes, take on seemingly impossible challenges and lead teams to victory over digital foes, are supplying people with the hit of satisfying hard work they need, giving them a purpose and a challenge and making them feel worthwhile, if only for a few hours a day. She quotes (rather large) figures for the typical number of hours US gamers spend online playing these types of game – 13 hours per week, by an estimated 183 million people. There are, according to McGonigal, 100 million regular gamers in Europe, 200 million in China and 105 million in India. People would much rather quest after imaginary trophies and dazzling jewels, fight tirelessly to slay virtual enemies, free captive team mates or dignitaries and continually attempt to 'level up' to the next set of challenges, seemingly not put off by repeated failures and the number of real-life hours lost to the virtual challenge.

What if, she suggests, we could use the elements and proven devices of games theory and design, not to simply create imaginary worlds where millions, if not billions of people, can lose themselves for hours at a time, but to create real-life social change? Imagine how powerful that could be? Harnessing the collective brain power and ingenuity of these eager 'warriors' and putting their combined effort to good, real, practical, positive use. It's an extremely powerful thought.

Indeed, this thought has already been put to the test through the phenomenally successful computer based *Foldit* experiment devised by medical researchers at the University of Washington. In 2011, would-be amateur science researchers around the world were challenged to attempt to decipher the protein structure of a monkey virus known to cause AIDS. Understanding and replicating this molecule was of critical importance to researchers in their fight to cure the disease. It attracted over 46,000 'players' who took part in the 'gameplay' over an originally timetabled, fixed period of three weeks. Participants received points for taking part and were awarded higher points the more complete and accurate their developed protein structure became. Remarkably, within just 10 days of the challenge, contributors had come up with an incredibly accurate model of the key enzyme that had kept professional medical researchers baffled for well over a decade.[18] This discovery has significantly advanced progress in the fight to defeat AIDS and it was achieved in less than a fortnight by a motley group of tens of thousands of unpaid, amateur enthusiasts – an impressive feat.

So, persuaded that this is an approach worth investigating further, how and where do you start to get your head around what a gamified approach to sustainability could look like?

What follows is a discussion of the various gamification 'Lego' bricks. We explore the building blocks of how it can be constructed, with the aim of giving you a simple 'starter guide' to the tricks and techniques behind bringing gamification into your business.

We start with a few basic definitions of common terms used in gamification theory such as social games, games mechanics and game design:

Social games

Social games are, at their simplest, games that are played with other people. Hence games such as Solitaire, Patience and Sudoku would not tend to fall into this category. Social games typically have the following characteristics:

ELEMENTS OF THE THEORY:
THE LEGO SET OF GAMIFICATION

- They have well-defined rules that must be followed

- They are for two or more players

- There is a pre-determined outcome or set of outcomes that signify the end of or stages in the game

- There is usually a winner (or at least an attainment of a certain level of the game by an individual or team)

- Each player has to expend effort of some type in playing the game

- Each player has a stake in the outcome of the game

Social games have a long history, with the earliest recorded dice games being found in Asia dating back to prehistory, and the first board game being found in a burial site in Egypt dating to circa 3500 BC. Another very early example of a social board game, the Royal Game of Ur, discovered by an explorer in the deserts of Iraq in the 1920s, seemingly a game played by Sumerian royalty and buried with them, can even be played online today at a British Museum website that has recreated it for a twenty-first-century gaming audience.[19]

Modern manifestations of social games are known as *social network games*, in other words, games that are typically played online through a social networking site. Social network games are some of the most popular games played in the world today with tens of millions of players, and some of their most famous incarnations are Happy Farm, Farm Ville and The Sims Social. Then there are the rather impressively titled 'Massively Multiplayer Online' (MMO) games, such as World of Warcraft which claims to be the biggest paying game community in the world with over 11.5 million registered players in 2010 (McGonigal, 2011).

One of the defining aspects of these multi-player games is that they engender a sense of 'community' even if this community is almost entirely virtual. The games tend to be shared by players through their online social networks, via Facebook, Bebo and the like. Hence the more popular games tend to quickly go 'viral' with little need for expensive, widespread marketing and PR campaigns.

The predominant route for 'gamification' solutions to date has been online and most recently the medium has developed further through the use of mobile apps. Some of the most popular games, however, are not necessarily completely novel nor indeed modern – for example, one very popular mobile app download is that most traditional of board games, Scrabble, which has been transformed for the twenty-first century by the idea of the scrabble board and letter counters being held in 'cloud', hence a game can be played between yourself and a cousin in Australia, for example, over an asynchronous time period that suits both parties.

Game mechanics

Game mechanics at their simplest are the 'rules and tools of engagement'. A defining element of what constituents a game is that it must have a number of rules, contrived boundaries or 'terms of engagement' by which would-be players voluntarily sign up to be constrained whilst playing. These can be simple, straightforward guidelines on the 'Dos and Don'ts' of the game, through to very complex, multi-layered instructions that reveal themselves as the game progresses or as you attain new levels. The various mechanics of the game can interact with each other to develop the level of complexity, and dictate the level of engagement of the players themselves.

Game design

The elements of game design are the true building blocks of a game, and they come together to form the gameplay and the mechanics/rules and give any particular game its unique character and feel. A number of the most common components of game design, and the elements most often seen in gamification techniques, are discussed below.

One size doesn't fit all

When planning a gamified process it is useful to think about categorising your potential audience into player types, a simple classification of the different general types of games players. This was originally derived by a UK-based games designer, Richard Bartle, who was a pioneer in the early development of multi-user dungeons, or MUDs. In reality, not as sinister as they may sound but simply the evolution of traditional games into online-based alternative virtual worlds that could be entered by many people to play with others from the comfort of their own desktops – the original online social media game format. From studying the users of MUDs, Bartle started to classify players into four main types:

- Achievers

- Explorers

- Socialisers

- Killers

Achievers: as the title suggest, this type of player wants to win. They want to master the game, they want to unlock the next level. They are interested in mastering new skills and hitting those targets and then moving on to the next challenge. This can be as an individual or within a team. Their main motivations are to overcome, get better, achieve and conquer the challenge.

Explorers: these are the curious. They enjoy the unlocking of new pathways, discovering hitherto unknown ways of playing and progressing; they like to understand the terrain and discover new techniques.

Socialisers: socialisers want to be liked. They are more interested in the team playing, sociable aspects of games and gaining the respect of their peer group. They will respond to more cause-based challenges. They often like to lead but to gain that position through popular vote.

Killers: for killers it's all about the competition. They really, really want to win. They want to beat the competition and see themselves topping the prize board. For killers all's fair in love, war and games.

Naturally, all games cannot appeal in equal measure to each of these broad categories, and an early consideration of your typical potential audience is useful in deciding what type of game mechanics you want to develop. However, if you can devise a gamified approach that appeals to at least two of these categories of player, you are widening the appeal of the challenge and encouraging broader participation.

How to 'gamify' a process

We have defined the various aspects of game development from which gamification derives. We now turn to the components of game design and describe some of the most common techniques used to 'gamify' processes. Sustainability-focused case studies are used to help to bring the elements to life and describe a real-life initiative where they have been utilised and results seen.

ELEMENTS OF THE THEORY:
THE LEGO SET OF GAMIFICATION

Fundamentally, a process is thought of as being 'gamified' if it exhibits at least one, but usually several, of the following features of game design:

Leader boards

Leader boards, or some other visual way of displaying the 'state of play' and the relative positions of the players/teams is useful for keeping people's interest and momentum up. If these boards can display in 'real time', or near to it, information on the relative progress of participants, so much the better as this has an instantly gratifying effect of keeping people involved, engaged and participating, whether it is to maintain their pole position, or to 'up their game' and push through the rankings. Human nature dictates that people like to see themselves as compared to others, hence where there is a competitive element and the chance of topping a 'league' in such a visual, public way, continued participation is enhanced.

Attainment levels ('levelling up')

Levelling up is an important concept in games mechanics and design, and is used frequently to reward sustained effort and ensure players do not lose interest as soon as they have conquered one level of the game. A well designed gamification intervention should have a number of levels or attainment stages to ensure enthusiasm and interest is maintained over time.

The term 'levelling up' has been adopted in the gaming world to describe the notion of working hard and persistently to beat the obstacles and challenges at a current level. In this sense, 'winning' is defined as completing that particular set of challenges or attaining a particular skill set, with the reward typically being the 'unlocking' of the next level of the game. The player then, in essence, heads straight back to a 'square one' position on the next, higher, typically more challenging level. The whole effort to 'level up' then starts again with renewed enthusiasm as new challenges present themselves.

Most of us can relate to the experience of being gripped by a desire to 'beat' a game, whether it be Tetris, Space Invaders, Angry Birds or a multitude of other ultimately pointless, but totally addictive, lone player games, only to lose interest completely the moment you 'conquer' that particular game. Without higher levels to master that replace the conquered task, then interest quickly wanes and it is typically not picked up again. Hence the importance of ensuring any challenge or competition is 'multi-levelled' in some respect in order to sustain enthusiasm and engagement over the longer term, but to also ensure that the increase in difficulty level is gradual so as not to turn players off by a sudden leap.

Rewards for effort expended

A key constituent of many successful online social media games and interactive membership-style sites is the idea of gaining 'rewards' in exchange for effort expended. These rewards do not necessarily have to be of a real cash value or indeed be real in any meaningful way. They do however need to be visible, and they require a 'value' in the eyes of the 'community' that needs to be easily communicated and recognised by others. This is illustrated by the plethora of online retail and other community-based sites where one earns 'rewards' in the shape of badges, stars, tokens, special privileges, etc. for engaging in some form of effort, assistance to others or focused activity. Online communities and shopping sites give rewards for user reviews of products purchased, events attended or experiences undertaken. Contribute enough of them, and you become a star member, your opinions valued more than the masses and hailed as a guru on the topic. For example, with Amazon, the reward for your reviewing efforts is to become a star reviewer and be featured on their site as such. Few of these rewards amount to much more than having a virtual gold star next to your username, but it is the kudos of achieving the status that drives members to expend much voluntary effort writing reviews or otherwise contributing time and energy to the cause.

Recognition badges

Following on from the idea of 'rewards', the achieving of certain levels, tasks, etc., are often recognised with an achievement badge. An old and well-established form of this is the idea of achieving activity badges in groups such as the Scouts and the Brownies, for example. Children proudly display their 'recognition of success' on the arms of their uniforms; the desire to attain these badges and, more importantly, display them to your peer group, is a powerful motivational tool.

Feedback loops

One of the key elements of a gamified process is the idea of constant and constructive feedback on effort undertaken and progress made. A manifestation of a feedback mechanism is the idea of a 'leader board' as described earlier, but feedback can and should go much further than that. Feedback on performance, given immediately after effort has been expended, for example in a points rating or qualitative ranking on this attempt as judged against an earlier effort, means that the individual can learn and act on the information in an immediate and positive way. Feedback, even when it is reporting back an ultimately failed endeavour, if given objectively and constructively, can encourage the player simply to try harder next time, getting back on that horse immediately after taking a tumble. A feedback mechanism that can capture any positive improvements, for example, a slightly faster time to completion, a higher total percentage rating or a generally more complete solution to the challenge, is also useful reinforcing the idea that each time a person tackles a task, they get better in some way, shape or form. This is a powerful motivational technique.

Eco case study: Fiat 500 eco driving[20] software

A good illustration on how feedback loops have been implemented successfully in the transport sector is the addition of eco-driving software and visualisation tools of performance in the dashboards of cars. The Fiat 500 has introduced a simple downloadable software solution called **eco:Drive**. The software is downloaded onto a computer and a USB stick is plugged into the dashboard; as the car is driven, information about the journey is captured. That data can be then uploaded onto a computer and the driver's style and performance analysed. The driver is given a score out of 100, the 'eco Index', for his/her effort on that occasion and given tips on how to improve next time (levelling up). There is a dashboard to monitor fuel and carbon saved, and to monitor personal performance and improvement over time. In addition, there is a function to set yourself challenges to improve your 'eco Index' by a self-selected value. There is also an online community of eco:Drive users – this community displays a cumulative score of total CO_2

saved by the entire community of Fiat ecoville members that, at the time of writing, weighed in at an impressive 4500 tonnes of CO_2 and has nearly 70,000 members. Fiat claims that drivers can save up to 15% on their fuel bills by using the app.

Credits

Similarly to rewards, the expending of effort and the achievement of certain tasks, or milestones can lead to the earning of credits and/or points. These can be real, i.e. to be spent on goods or services; or virtual, in terms of buying more privileges within a game. A number of successful environmentally focused initiatives rely on the idea of people earning 'credits' for good work done, for example in recycling their rubbish, that they can then go on to spend in the high street. Crucially, this type of credit is not awarded for simply buying more stuff at a particular supermarket, or only buying fuel from a certain chain of petrol stations – that type of approach is simply a straightforward loyalty or incentive scheme. Instead, these gamified processes require action, effort and/ or behavioural change to be rewarded with credit. Recyclebank is a well-established example of this type of gamification technique.

Eco case study: Recyclebank

Recyclebank originated in the United States and is now available in the UK. They claim to have four million members worldwide. It is a credit-based initiative that rewards people who join the scheme and register their recycling and other pro-environmental efforts with credits that can then be spent in participating retailers and other service providers on the high street. The more they participate, and the more friends they recruit, the more points they receive. Alternatively, people can donate their credits to a number of approved schools projects, where Recyclebank turns the points into a cash donation to the school.

Peer-to-peer comparison

The need to compare oneself with one's neighbour, work colleague, family member or another in one's social circle is innate – the idea of 'keeping up with the Jones's' hasn't remained a well-worn cliché for so long without good reason! In the absence of any other metrics by which to measure social standing or level of expertise in a subject or activity – the comparison with someone you recognise as your equal more generally is an important benchmark.

This type of technique must be used with caution however, as if the comparison is too broad or general or deemed irrelevant – for example, a national average, sector average or if perceived not to reflect the individual's own view of themselves – there is a risk they will not engage or switch off from the process entirely. A useful illustration of how this gamification technique has been deployed in the environmental sector, with varying degrees of success, is discussed next.

Eco case study: Act on CO_2 Carbon Calculator Comparator Tool

An early output of the UK government's general climate change education and communication campaign, Act on CO_2 was an online, interactive, engagement tool – the Act on CO_2 Carbon Calculator.[21] This footprinting calculator was developed for the domestic sector and its original aims were: to increase carbon literacy throughout the British public; allow citizens to calculate their own household and/or individual carbon footprint arising from their use of energy/ transport fuels; and to provide users with a personalised action plan to assist in engagement with energy efficient activities to reduce their carbon footprint. It provided an instant feedback mechanism in that as soon as the user had input energy and fuel usage data, they received their carbon footprint value. Users were then encouraged to do a peer-to-peer comparison through comparing their measured footprint to a 'National Average' foot-print value, derived through taking the total emissions for the domestic sector and dividing that by the number of households in the UK. The calculator proved to be popular and received over a million visits in the first year with a completion rate of around 40%.

However, research into the user experience of interacting with the calculator and the potential for it being a behavioural change tool brought interesting unforeseen consequences to light. Users, after completing their footprint, were encouraged to explore the results section of the website to help them put their footprint value into context. They then explored the 'call to action' features, which consisted of a dynamically generated, personalised action plan, predicated on their answers, with the intention of encouraging them to take up the suggested pro-environmental actions. The functionality that allowed comparison of an individual's footprint result with that of the national average uncovered two curiously challenging issues. The first insight was that a number of users, who saw their footprints were higher than the national average carbon footprint, became dismissive and defensive when confronted with this unfavourable comparison. They maintained they could not be compared to the national average, as they and their lifestyles/family situations were not 'average' and hence the comparator was not valid; in other words they were not prepared to accept the tool as a true peer-to-peer comparator and so dismissed the result. Instead, they maintained, if they could only be compared to 'people like themselves' – with similar homes, family size, lifestyle, etc., then that would be a more accurate and subsequently relevant comparison tool.

The second issue to emerge was that some users who came in lower than the national average could express a tendency to be complacent with their current score. Hence they felt they could disengage with the notion of further action to reduce their carbon footprint as they were already doing 'better than the average' and so felt they had 'done their bit' for the environment.

This posed a dilemma for the project team, as it was important that the calculator, as well as being an educational tool and a visually engaging way of explaining a carbon footprint, was also a tool for further engagement and pro-environmental behavioural change.

The addition of the peer comparison with a nationally derived average value, was in some cases (but not by any means all), disappointingly proving a disincentive to further action.

However, after over two years of use, the tool had collected approximately one million sets of carbon footprints from a wide range of household sizes and types, and this raised the possibility of developing a 'people like me' style comparator tool,[22] based on the totally anonymised dataset, which could potentially overcome the issue of users who initially disregarded the national average comparison. This functionality was developed and released in a second edition. Early user testing research revealed that this type of highly personalised peer-to-peer comparator functionality resonated more strongly with users. It also removed a particular barrier to action in the subset of users who disengaged primarily because they did not feel the national average comparator was appropriate or useful for them.

The learning from this case study is that a peer-to-peer comparator can be a very powerful tool in gamification processes, but the comparison metrics must be felt to be appropriate by its intended audience, otherwise it may have the unintended, contrary effect of disengaging the exact audience it was meant to engage.

Public pledges

Pledges, resolutions or promises, whether made in a public way or not, have been a mainstay of environmental and health-related campaigns for many years, with, to be frank, mixed levels of success. An important key to ensuring that any promise or pledge is adhered to is to ensure they are made in a way that is available to significant others, whether family, friends, community group or work/teammates, to view and informally 'police' through peer pressure.

Publicly made declarations of intent, or pledges, especially if made to assist or help others, have the most likely chances of success. The impression that you would be letting others down if you break your pledge, as opposed to simply letting yourself down, is a much more powerful motivator, and suggests that it could act as a powerful driver to keep someone on the straight and narrow, more than individual willpower alone.

Eco case study: The DoNation

A novel form of 'pledging' for pro-environmental actions can be seen in the innovative, cashless sponsorship website platform The DoNation.[23] The DoNation takes the well-established idea of sponsoring friends and family to perform various heroic deeds of athleticism such as running a marathon or completing a triathlon, but instead of the person asking for money, they ask their friends, families and colleagues to sponsor them in simple sustainability actions with the metric of saved carbon emissions as the quantifiable 'score'. The number and types of actions, or 'DoActions' as they are called on the site, that have been pledged are added to the sponsored person's public 'totaliser' page on the website and the accumulated amount of carbon saved by all the pledgees is calculated and displayed.

This is a very public and permanent display of the pledgees and their pledges made. In addition, typically, as the group of people sponsoring an individual are usually part of either a tightly or loosely knit peer group – as at the very least, they all have the sponsored person in common, the obligation to actually carry out your pledged action is felt more strongly by the individual – they don't want to be the one that is seen to be 'letting the side down', especially if the person they sponsored has successfully completed their challenge. They are also encouraged to return to the site after two months, to declare they have competed their actions – a useful extra 'nudge' or 'incentive' to remind people to complete their chosen 'DoAction'.

A survey conducted in January 2013, involving a range of the people raising sponsorship and their 'Doers', showed that 77% of the pledgers said they felt more committed to keeping their pledge because it was personal, in support of a friend or a team they were part of. On the sponsored person side, 67% said they were motivated to keep to the challenge and train harder. Sixty-one per cent of pledgers said they were thinking about doing the actions already, but this scheme gave them the nudge they needed to actually get on and do them.[24] Finally and crucially, 41% reported that they realised that doing the green thing isn't as unappealing and boring as they had previously imagined, and that 81% of the Doers were planning to keep up their actions long term.

Competitive element

There usually is a 'winner' in a gamified process, as the idea of winning appeals to a competitive spirit that is to a greater or lesser extent inherent in all of us. However, it can be quite a loosely defined term within the overall package and its terms of importance can be downplayed compared to the significance and kudos of 'taking part' and/or being part of a team. The winner can be an individual, a team, department, or whole office; indeed the 'winner' can be the entire community of players if they are all coming together to achieve an 'epic win'. It is important however, to devise a mechanism that doesn't simply reinforce existing notions of what defines the 'high achievers' in a company or community, or that could lead to a situation where the 'usual suspects' always come out on top, leading to disenchantment and disengagement in the process. It is also important to decide exactly what constitutes a 'winner' and how they are selected, and how the field can be opened up again at every stage of the challenge.

A number of these techniques are certainly not new. Indeed rewards, credits and prizes for loyalty and repeat purchases are a mainstay of 'incentive' and 'loyalty' schemes the world over from AirMiles, Nectar points and the Green Shield stamps of old. And indeed, some loyalty schemes are now rebranding themselves as 'gamified processes' in order to jump on the gamification bandwagon. However, it can be argued that straightforward incentive-based and purchasing loyalty schemes are not examples of a gamified process as there is no evidence of the 'satisfying hard work', a key focus for McGonigal's definition, as discussed at the start of this chapter.

If you want to start to gamify an idea, or if you are seeking direction on some key indicators to guide you in the consideration of whether something can be considered 'gamified', here is a list of key questions to keep in mind:

- Does the application promote active intervention, engagement and effort by the people involved?

- Are there well-defined rules of engagement and boundaries?

- Are there opportunities to improve, and is there useful and timely feedback, to the 'players' involved?

- Is there a method of keeping track of how the individual players, and/or the team, are doing in comparison with other participants?

- Is there an 'end game' of sorts? Is there a winner, or winning team?

- Are people having fun?

If you can answer yes to two or more of these questions, then you can consider your endeavour to have been gamified.

CHAPTER 3

Gamification for Sustainability: Can 'Fun and Games' Really Save the Planet?

WE HAVE DISCUSSED WHERE the concept of gamification originated. We've explored the building blocks of what a 'gamified' process could contain and looked at a number of examples of where individual elements of it have been implemented successfully in the sustainability space.

We move on in this chapter to debate what potential gamification might have to re-invigorate the rather moribund debate in the environmental and sustainability sector about how to motivate, inspire and change habits and behaviours in mainstream society. Can it help us reach recalcitrant work colleagues, or the hard-to-reach sectors of society, who have been put off or alienated from more environmentally friendly lifestyle choices by the tone and nature of the messages being broadcast?

This chapter will explore this, the fundamental question of the book: whether 'fun and games' can really help save the planet. Or is the entire theory just mere 'bagatelle'?

Various methods of behaviour change intervention have so far had limited success in motivating wider society into taking positive environmental actions. In the face of constant bombardment of messages regarding ice

GAMIFICATION FOR SUSTAINABILITY:
CAN 'FUN AND GAMES' REALLY SAVE THE PLANET?

caps melting, sea levels rising, polar bears drowning, exceptional droughts, one hundred-year storm occurrences becoming more frequent, resource depletion and habitat destruction, it is surprising that still a majority of the population do nothing more in this area than put the recycling out once a week and buy fair trade bananas from their local supermarket.

As we discussed in Chapter 1, one of the theories for why people refuse to change their lifestyles and habits in the face of mounting evidence of harm is that, in the case of climate change in particular, the issue is too disparate, difficult to pinpoint and, despite the efforts of hundreds of the world's best climate scientists, still considered uncertain as to the causes. In addition, the potential effects of a warming world are still too distant in both space and time to galvanise immediate action by individuals. If this is the case, and there is little in the short term that can be done about these opinions and attitudes, then there has to be another route to persuade people to change the way they live to become less resource-intensive and carbon-footprint-heavy.

Enter gamification. Although gamification is still a new concept, it has been adopted by some forward thinkers in the sustainability space and tested through a range of applications. To date, as the previous case studies in Chapter 2 has highlighted, these have tended to concentrate on the home and the individual, for example, educating people to use less energy, recycle more, drive more efficiently and even to not throw rubbish and inappropriate objects down the toilet.[25] However, there is much opportunity to further develop gamified processes, products and ways of working that will benefit employees, the business and its bottom line more generally, and this is what we explore in the remainder of the book with the existing pioneers in this sector.

HOW GAMIFICATION CAN HELP YOUR BUSINESS ENGAGE IN SUSTAINABILITY

We now live in an era where embracing sustainability commercially is now accepted as a viable, cost-effective route to opening up new markets and customers, to gaining stakeholder trust, and it has become one of the core pillars for non-financial metrics reporting in the corporate world. However, in recent times discussions have focused on the challenge of maintaining such a sustainability vision to transform, for the long term, the way employees, customers and shareholders engage with the concept.

In particular, the notion of harnessing the power of the collective through ongoing, multi-levelled challenges and competition is a potentially very exciting idea for proponents and practitioners of environmental sustainability and behaviour change programmes, many of whom are craving new, engaging ways in which to reach out to a wider audience than the 'usual suspects' of green-minded individuals within an organisation, business or community.

At the community level, it could provide an alternative approach to engaging local people in activities and campaigns, people who may historically have been turned off by the overtly 'green', 'eco' or 'save the planet' messaging that green advocates and evangelists tend to enthusiastically espouse.

At the business level it provides an additional, novel way of involving staff in environmental employee engagement – taking such schemes out of the 'Green Champion'/'Environmental Rep' silo that some well-intentioned, but limited, initiatives have had a tendency to fall into over recent years. The wider appeal of a challenge or competition-based approach has the potential to enthuse a much broader spectrum of workers to take part in such schemes. It appeals to the innate, competitive instincts of humans and can potentially provide powerful motivations to kick-start programmes of long-term organisational behavioural change with multiple levels of engagement and complexity to suit all-comers. So, let's take a look at how gamification can provide a new route into encouraging people to change their habits.

We have already suggested that one reason why more people do not take up the challenge of mitigating climate change is that they feel powerless in the face of such an overwhelming problem. It can appear that individual action is ultimately ineffectual and a bit of a waste of time. 'Why bother trying to cut down on my household's electricity bill to reduce my footprint when China is building a new coal powered station every five days' is an oft-quoted excuse for apathy and inaction.

One obvious pathway out of this inaction is to show people that they are making a difference, they can make an impact; maybe not individually, but as part of a work team, community group, virtual crowd, neighbourhood, nation, whatever. This is where the power of games comes into its own.

McGonigal in her book talks about the idea of an 'engagement economy', creating a group or community, where there may have been nothing there before, to come together to achieve something concrete, whether it be a goal to reach, a challenge to overcome or a quantity of tasks to achieve. She argues the way to do this is to give the group a challenge, turn it into a competition and give regular feedback on how the individual, as well as the 'engaged group' as a whole, is doing. This is the essence of what gamification does. It can turn a relatively mundane task into an adventure. It gives people the *purpose* and the *challenge* they need to get motivated and involved; regular *feedback* gives them information and encouragement on what their *impact* is and how much *progress* they are making (and if they aren't, encouragement to help make them 'up their effort'); it shows them how they are doing in *comparison* with others and showing that there is the possibility of *success*, however huge the challenge.

As they say, 'it ain't rocket science', and we're not revealing anything you didn't instinctively know already, but it's the neat encapsulation of these elements in a gamified process that gives it its novelty and power.

So, the fundamentals of how to gamify a process can be displayed in this flow diagram:

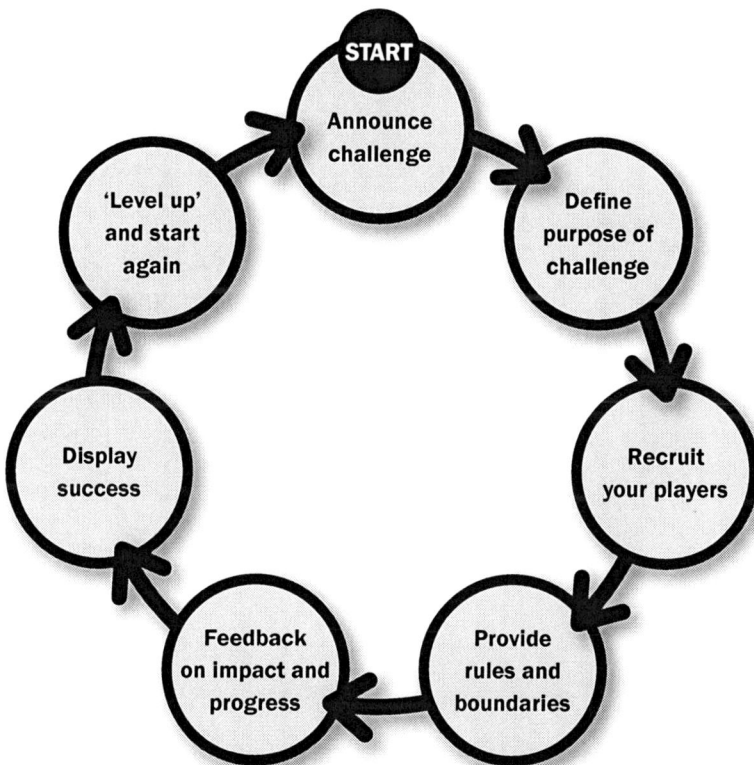

GAMIFICATION FOR SUSTAINABILITY:
CAN 'FUN AND GAMES' REALLY SAVE THE PLANET?

Giving people the sense that they are not in it alone is important. That their individual effort, albeit tiny in isolation, when seen in context with the efforts of many other, like-minded souls, does actually make a significant impact is enough to dissipate the inertia and helplessness of the individual and turn them into a competitive 'eco-warrior'. This type of call to action appeals to the Explorers and the Socialisers in our groups (the Bartle player types discussed in Chapter 2). Throw a little healthy competition into the mix for the Achievers and Killers amongst us and you have a powerful engagement tool and behaviour change driver.

Yes, the challenge of mitigating climate change is still of epic proportions, and, yes, the individual's contribution to the solution is still tiny in isolation, but large, audacious challenges are taken every single day, by regular, everyday people the world over. You only have to see the rise in the popularity of marathon running, by seemingly ordinary folk who had never run for the bus before taking up the challenge, and succeeding at it, to realise that if the challenge, motivation, feedback and competition is set at the right level, anything is possible.

Hence, we postulate, it's worth giving the ideas and techniques of gamification a 'go' in the sustainability space. Basically what have we got to lose?

....

CHAPTER 4

Eco-Gamification in Business: How is it Playing Out?

NOW THAT THE FUNDAMENTALS of gamification and its mechanisms have been explained, I will make a wager with you that you will begin to see elements of gamification in play everywhere. Take the market-leading business networking site LinkedIn[26] for example.

Although LinkedIn could not be described as a gaming site (despite the fact that some users seem to approach collecting as many contacts, known to them or not, as an informal competition), it has over recent years introduced a number of gamification elements to safeguard loyalty and frequent repeat visits to the site by its members. You may have noticed the introduction of a 'progress bar' which monitors the percentage completeness of your profile. It persistently encourages you to come back and add more detail with the ultimate goal of 'scoring' 100%, an example of using feedback loops and attainment levels to keep motivation and engagement high. More recently, it has introduced the idea of peer-voted recognition badges in the form of 'endorsements' of your stated skill and experience set. It is a form of 'plus 1' point scoring and acts as a public endorsement, by the people who matter to you professionally, of your abilities, talents and reputation in your sector. This is a clever feature that has introduced a whole new level of engagement with the site by playing to people's professional pride, need for positive feedback and craving for public recognition.

Aside from LinkedIn there are more examples of gamification being embraced, and in the sustainable business sector in particular, to help engage staff, communities and others. We explore a range of them here (due to the space restrictions of this book we can only discuss a few) and have concentrated on those that have proven results. However, we provide a longer list of examples of environmentally focused games and gamification applications in the further reading section at the end of this book.

Employee engagement

An early mover in this area is the sustainability software company CloudApps.[27] CloudApps provide a full sustainability reporting software solution. No new innovation there as performance reporting software has permeated the market steadily over recent years with the advent of the CRC, but where CloudApps has snatched early mover market advantage is their new employee engagement tool SuMo (short for SUstainabilty MOmentum) in which they have merged sustainability, games mechanics, social networking and gamification in one mobile software package.

Cloudapps' SuMo product claims to be bringing an average 9% reduction in annual travel costs to their customers as well as aligning staff to the company's sustainability vision and goals in a more engaging and satisfying way. The building blocks of gamification are all present and correct. SuMo uses elements of design and mechanics including challenges, levelling up, gold badges and recognition through the use of leader boards. An illustration of the SuMo interface, which displays a dashboard-style personalised performance tracker, is reproduced in Figure 1.

FIGURE 1. Dashboard for ClouApps SuMo employee engagement software tool.

Another similar product for employee engagement has been created by the British company ecoinomy.[28] They produce a number of products, suitable for small or larger companies, which provide the platform and mechanics to engage staff in environmental actions, with the rewards of these actions going to a cause of the employees' choice.

A recent case study involves the work they undertook with the energy company SSE. The company used the product eco.system. Eco. system is implemented in larger office environments and works over the internet using social network principles. Each participating employee has their own online account and when they spot an opportunity to bring about a change in the workplace they enter the action into the system. An example would be sharing a lift with a colleague rather than using separate vehicles. The amount of money and CO_2 saved by the action is logged by the system, using pre-configured data, and the benefits apportioned to the employee.

SSE used the system to engage staff in eco-saving behaviours, with the motivation being that a proportion of the monetary savings made could be shared with the community causes that the staff had chosen.

A workshop was held to identify what the staff thought would be useful to concentrate on and that would reduce costs, waste and increase performance. Actions included: switching things off at night; reducing business travel and printing; trying out their own eco-saving ideas; and arriving at meetings on time.

Monetary values were given to the actions, and the staff involved were encouraged to form fundsaving guilds: these were self-forming teams that decided to give their rewards to a local cause.

Results were impressive. Over one quarter of all staff at the site joined in with the scheme. The trial saved £41,000 in costs and 66 tonnes of CO_2. An annualised estimate of the savings for each employee active in the scheme came to £350; this translates to a potential £7 million saved if every employee in SSE took up the challenge in the future. Over £8000 were donated to local causes and nearly 5000 actions undertaken.

Waste and recycling

Another example of community engagement tools and solutions can be found in the Borough of Bexley, London. The council partnered with the ethical eco-living company Green Rewards to trial a pilot scheme that had a goal of improving recycling rates across the borough.

The initial pilot lasted for one year and involved 2000 households across Bexley and in the summer of 2012 was extended to another 13,000 purpose-built flats in the area. The aims of the scheme were to incentivise residents to reduce the amount of rubbish they sent for disposal by reducing, re-using and recycling their waste and to tackle the problem of fly-tipping in the area. The households were recruited in geographically close 'communities' and were challenged collectively to reduce the amount of landfill waste they generated. Each participating household was given an account, provided with a membership card and key fob (see Figure 2) and could track progress both online and offline (to avoid excluding any older and/or non-internet using households). They were given points for effort and reductions in landfill waste collections, measured by reductions in total weight of the community collection, the measurements were reported quarterly and all participating households were rewarded equally if there was an improvement in their area's rates. These could be spent at the Green Rewards website[29] on environmentally friendly products. Alternatively they could donate their points to one of three self-designated local charities.

Results are impressive. In total, the trial garnered 18% participation overall, but reached 29% in the first, smaller phase. Although the scheme was created to work best online – as regular updates and other news and reporting could be 'pushed' easily to the participants – the trial found that 57% of accounts are managed online, and 43% offline. Hence the importance of considering all forms of engagement and communication, both offline as well as online, when planning a wide community participation scheme.

....

FIGURE 2. London Green Points Bexley membership card.

....

Participating households also received general updates on the scheme every quarter alongside broader hints and tips on living a more sustainable lifestyle. The membership card also extended to include incentives and discounts at a range of local independent shops and businesses to promote more local participation in the area. It is still early days in the reporting of reductions in the amount of waste to landfill through the pilot scheme, although the Council has reported the preliminary findings of reductions in residual waste amounts of around 24% when compared to the year before (September–November 2011 to September–November 2012).

The scheme has proved its popularity sufficiently enough to be rolled out to 52,000 households in the wider vicinity. In addition, the Royal Borough of Greenwich, Rother District Council and Gloucestershire County Council are currently working on plans with Local Green Points to introduce similar schemes and initiatives in 2013.

Energy use

Across the pond the ideas of using friendly competition and neighbourly rivalry have been utilised in a scheme to encourage householders to reduce their energy consumption. The US-based software company OPower has been working with utility companies in the States since 2007, using techniques such as behavioural norms and peer-to-peer comparisons to encourage people to understand their energy bills and ultimately, reduce their consumption. In five years they have grown into a company employing 250 people and are working with around 70 energy utility companies. They claim to have reached over 10 million homes across America and to have helped save a tetrawatt of energy by 2012.

HOW GAMIFICATION CAN HELP YOUR BUSINESS
ENGAGE IN SUSTAINABILITY

OPower began its consumer-based energy efficiency behavioural pro-grammes with a simple idea of bringing energy use, and utility bills, to life for ordinary citizens. Aided significantly in the US by the availability of accessible individual household energy consumption data to a neighbourhood level, OPower set about using a peer-to-peer comparison game mechanic to engage people in a competition of energy consumption reduction. They worked with utility companies to add metrics to bills that showed households how they compared to an average, anonymised consumption rate of their neighbourhood. But in addition to the neighbourhood comparator metric they also provided help and advice on how the householder could 'level up', to increase their ranking by using less energy. They report, on average, that they help to save householders 2% on their energy bills simply by showing them the comparison to their neighbours' bills. Translated to a UK context, and taking the average gas and electricity bill in 2012,[30] this would amount to an approximate household saving of £25, and scaled up to national level could account for a cumulative £700 million saving.

In spring 2012 they took the idea of the social interaction element of energy consumption a step further by launching a mobile app[31] in conjunction with Facebook. This allowed users to share their actual consumption data with friends and families. Taking it up a level from viewing anonymised averaged consumption figures from their local neighbourhood, here they could actually see consumption levels of their chosen peer group, and challenge them to a competition to lower it. The can also compete in challenges, earn points and badges, and participate in community groups. Wayne Lin, Opower's social product manager, noted in an article in a Deloitte review that 'our goal is to foster an environment where people talk about their energy use in ways their friends can relates to. And through that, we encourage people to find ways to save electricity.' As it is still relatively early days in the project, there are no reports on levels of take up or success metrics in terms of energy consumption reduction; however, OPower reported in August 2012 that 17 of its existing utility partners had already engaged with the application.

In the summer of 2012, OPower opened its first international office in London and has teamed up with an independent utility suppler, First Utility, to trial this gamification-led behavioural programme in the UK for the first time.[32]

Quality of life

A more systemic, holistic gamification application can be illustrated by studying the online game Mindbloom Life. Mindbloom is aimed at inspiring people to define what aspects of life are important to them, discover what motivates them and encourage them to go out and live the life they crave by rewarding them for doing good things. It takes the metaphor of the tree of life and you earn points and credits by completing positive actions, which then translate into sunlight and water that makes your tree thrive – so far, so hippy! But what MindBloom does differently is to harness the tricks of the gamifying trade to make this 'quality of life' type application an example of the gamification of life itself.

Mindbloom is a veteran of the gamification application as it was created back in 2008. The game was trialled for one year. At the close of the trial approximately 1.3 million actions were committed to, with 1.2 million of them being tagged as completed. The company launched a mobile version of its successful pc-based programme in 2011 (known as

Bloom*) and is now being rolled out to all the employees and customers of Aetna, a major health care benefits company in the US. Aetna claim to serve nearly 35 million people with information and resources to help them live healthier lives, and hence this could represent the biggest potential audience for a gamification application to date.[33]

Transportation

Moving continents to Asia now, we see an innovative programme trialled in Bangalore, the INSTANT project,[34] that was devised to address the severe and persistent issue of congestion and increased commuting times over peak rush hour periods in the city. The high-tech boom through the twenty-first century has seen the population of Bangalore almost double and the spread of the city increase threefold; however, this increase in population has not included an upgrading of the city's transport infrastructure and congestion and pollution issues have become more acute over this time period.

Infosys technologies, the company involved in the programme, was motivated into action through a double incentive of reducing both lost time and money spent on fuel. The company bussed in many of its workers each morning, and found over time that buses were spending an extra 40 minutes on the roads and the additional fuel wasted was costing the company $300 per day.

The INSTANT project, a collaboration between Stanford University researchers and Infosys, experimented with a scheme that incentivised workers with credits, depending on what time the employee swiped-in on arrival. A pre-8.30 a.m. arrival time was rewarded with a credit for the draw, and the more times this occurred, the more chance they had of winning the monthly prize draw. The gamification mechanisms involved were the idea of a reward pyramid (different rewards with different credits), time-based credit allocation, weekly draws and credit deduction. The final mechanism implies that after every draw, a number of credits are deducted from the winners; this is to allow other participants the chance to win future prizes and to encourage a steady participation.

The results of the experiment were impressive. There was a doubling of workers who arrived for work before 8 a.m., hence avoiding the worst of the rush hour congestion. The company's bus shuttle fleet could be deployed more effectively and reduce its fuel use and they found generally that commuting time decreased from 71 minutes to 54 minutes on average.[35] The scheme, whilst it was running, resulted in a net saving of 2600 person-hours per day at the Infosys factory site.

To add a cautionary end note to this case study, the researchers have found that since the end of the experiment workers start times and commuting times have started to creep up again. As the experiment was performed over a six-month period, it could be assumed that this lapsed timescale is long enough to ensure that newly formed commuting patterns would become habits that would continue beyond the existence of the monthly incentive of the prize draw. However, if the reward for involvement was simply monetary in scope, and not engaging with the more intrinsic rewards that are mooted as being so important within the gamification field, then that might explain the lack of continued participation by some commuters once the monetary reward was taken away.

In the same vein, more recently Stanford researchers teamed up with Singapore's Land Transport Authority (LTA), to launch another pilot scheme entitled Insinc. Insinc encourages participating commuters to shift their commute schedules on the Singapore rail system away from overcrowded peak times. The more commuters participate in Insinc, the more opportunities they would unlock to receive random rewards. The system gave higher value points depending on the time shift of the journey, for example, if the journey was shifted to a designated 'decongesting' time period then commuters could win extra points as compared to travelling at peak times. Insinc aims to reduce crowded trains by distributing the load, resulting in a more efficient use of Singapore's transportation resources. Insinc was launched in January 2012 to study the effects of incentives and social interaction on public transit commuting. The pilot trial ended in July 2012, with $330,000 paid out in rewards and thousands of commuters taking part in the scheme. LTA has decided to continue the Insinc study for another 18 months.

CHAPTER 5

Conclusion:
Are You Game?

WE HAVE NOW EXAMINED the ideas behind gamification, considered building blocks of what it contains and looked at some examples of how it is playing out in the sustainability sector in this early stage of its evolution. Now we are coming to the end game, it's time to take a look at how companies could potentially use the concept and techniques to create their own gamified projects.

How to play the game

The first step in any such initiative is to have a clearly defined brief of what you want it to achieve. The goal could be large and organisation-wide. For example, the UK government, through its 'Greening Government' project, requires all non-governmental public bodies (NGPBs) to reduce their carbon footprint by 25%, reduce waste to landfill by 25% and reduce business-related transport by 15%, all by 2015. These are big, scary figures but useful long-term goals to be aiming at. Such large, distant targets will need to be broken down into more manageable slices, but it is quite useful to have an ultimate goal in place in order to give a suitably challenging ambition for staff to engage with.

Or alternatively it could start as a challenge between individuals, teams, entire floors or offices to reduce their use of power, water, waste or paper for example, the most in a specified short timescale. Ultimately, your goal is the same, an overall reduction in resource use by the organisation as a whole over a period of time, but this is framing it as a competition from the start.

Once the ultimate goal is defined, you then have to design the mechanics of how the initiative will play out. To begin with you need a starting point, a baseline with which to record progress and award points, credits and prizes. This is the 'base level' or 'level zero' and is where all 'players' will start and progress and achievements calculated.

Then you need to define the mechanics of the 'game'. What are the rules, boundaries and terms of engagement that staff will need to voluntarily sign up to if they are to take part? Will there be winners – and are they to be individual, team or office based? How and by what metrics are they decided upon? Will there be different stages of the competition, so players can 'level up' once they have achieved certain initial goals and skills?

How will the initiative be played out? Will it be administered totally online (however, heeding the cautionary lesson about participation levels both online and offline in the Bexley Council case study on page 182 in Chapter 4)? Or is it something you will manage using offline scoring and communication tools? Or a combination of both?

If it is going to be an initiative that people engage with online, then the development of a web-based dashboard to keep score and return feedback will need to be developed or purchased. This can be quite costly and/or time-consuming and must be factored into the budget and timelines before you start. Offline-based initiatives are easier and simpler to get off the ground, but less sophisticated in their reporting and feedback mechanisms.

Once these initial questions are answered the fun can begin! The next stage is the creation of the game itself and the development of the mechanics, design elements and the gameplay of your challenge.

We will continue this discussion using a simple example to make it more real-world. We will consider creating a company-wide employee engagement project with the aim of reducing the total amount of waste and recycling thrown out by an office-based organisation over a specified period of time.

For example, we shall fix that the ultimate goal is to reduce waste that goes to landfill by 50% in a 12-month period. As landfill waste incurs a premium charge of £64 per tonne, and this is increasing by £8 each year in line with the landfill tax duty escalator, this challenge has a very readily quantifiable monetary saving target as well as the obvious wider environmental benefits.

A baseline to the total amount of waste disposed of, both landfill residual waste and any recyclate materials, should be easily obtained from the waste disposal company as companies are typically charged either by weight or volume of waste arising. A trickier job is to calculate a typical per floor, or area, amount of waste disposed of, so teams can be pitted against one another to reduce the most. This can be done by designating a typical week to monitor a baseline and recruiting a team of volunteers (usually green reps if the company already has them), or instructing the cleaning staff to measure the amount of waste collected per area at the end of each working day.

Then the challenge begins. Employees are encouraged to join teams that are physically close to where they typically sit. The total baseline for the organisation is announced and the first level challenge is announced – which team can make the biggest percentage reduction in their area's waste to landfill in a designated week, for example. Additionally, there could be an open competition for everyone to submit suggestions for the quirkiest re-use of office materials to remove them from the waste stream entirely, the winner being put to a public vote.

Ideally for the week of measuring, the waste from each area should be weighed internally – this will give a regular feedback mechanism. However, the overall reduction in waste can be gained from the waste company, who typically measure it through the number of bags they collect, rather than weight, but the figures may not be obtained that frequently and will only give the total reduction, not split by floor, or area.

A first winning team is announced, and the leader board unveiled. The next level of challenge is then revealed: the first team to cut their waste to landfill by a further 50%. And so on. Until the final challenge, a zero landfill waste week, for example. In this challenge, everyone pulls together for a short designated time period to see if it is possible to achieve – the 'epic win' in gamification parlance. The individual challenges, such as best individual idea for waste reduction and the most innovative re-use ideas, would also receive prizes.

The challenge would close with the unveiling of both the total amount of waste saved from landfill, the parallel reduction in recycled materials in general and the total money saved from landfill tax levy and reduced disposal volumes. A proportion of this saving could be then used to reward staff in some way, or be awarded to local charities or other community causes nominated by the staff who took part.

If this challenge is undertaken over a period of months, and the communication of both the monetary and environmental benefits clearly and effectively communicated alongside the achievements of the teams and the individual prize winners, then ideally the new waste-saving habits of the staff will now be seen as the new 'norm' with the company.

Levelling up in this case can mean another round of waste reducing challenges, or the competition can move on to similar tasks surrounding the use of electricity in the office, the amount of paper consumed, a 'switch off' challenge, a commuting-related task, business travel challenge or any other number of areas you might want to tackle.

These are the simplest type of gamified interactions. Once these are played out, how about increasing the stakes and looking to your supply chain, or in the case of manufacturing, how you produce your product and look to gamify improvements in production methods. Once you start thinking about what can be turned into a challenge or competition of some description, the ideas will flow.

This type of challenge has been designed to appeal to various categories of players as defined by Bartle, and described on page 158 in Chapter 2. The idea of having particular goals to achieve and targets to hit will appeal to the Achiever category. The working in teams to achieve the reduction needed and gain money for a chosen charity will be the hook for the Socialisers in the team, as well as the final challenge of getting everyone to work together to produce zero waste. The Explorers will respond to the competition of creating new and innovative ways of reducing the waste arising and re-using resources in novel ways. And finally Killers – well, if Killers join in, they will be just there to win it at all costs, but this challenge might not be competitive enough for them to be particularly engaged. Still, three out of four ain't bad.

A 10-step checklist to gamifying your business processes:

Step 1: Define your main objective(s) for this challenge

Step 2: Calculate your starting point

Step 3: Define the overall goal – helps if this is a quantified target and even more so if it has quantified monetary value

Step 4: Decide how the project will play out (is it going to be a one hit to get things moving, or are you going to introduce various levels to achieve over time, to ultimately secure the overall goal)

Step 5: Choose your gamification building blocks (from the selection in Chapter 3)

Step 6: Develop the mechanics of the programme

Step 7: Communicate the messages to staff

Step 8: Launch the challenge/competition

Step 9: Give regular and encouraging feedback, introduce leader boards, points, intermediate prizes

Step 10: Announce winner(s), and prepare to level up.

We have now come to the end of this brief tour around the brave new world of 'fun and games' for sustainability, which leaves just a few closing comments to be made. These are still early days for the whole concept of gamification, particularly in the sustainability field, and it still has to prove its staying power as a useful engagement tool. Some initiatives have already proved to be impactful in their early-reported successes, but we will need the perspective of time to tell if they have any longevity in terms of lasting attitude, belief and behaviour change however the early signs are positive.

Predictably however, given the rising amount of attention that the topic is getting, a backlash has already started within the blogosphere and beyond regarding the current implementation of gamification. Accenture,[36] in a recent report on gamification and behaviour change, describe the views of critics that argue the representation of gamification as it currently stands is too simplistic, too narrow a focus on what gamification can be and too 'narrow an ambition regarding what use of games can achieve'.

Interestingly however, the tone of this backlash, at least as described by the Accenture report, is not rubbishing the concept of gamification itself. Instead it is criticising the supposedly limited (in ambition at least) implementation of its true potential to date. This, to us at least, sounds more positive than negative. If what the critics say has substance, then we can imagine that we are currently looking at 'Level 1' in the game of gamification in its wider applications. Once we have mastered the basic tools and skills needed to gamify processes as the term is currently understood, we will have the opportunity to 'level up' to the next set of more ambitious gamifying challenges. What could be more appropriate than gamifying gamification itself?

This is the beginning of the gamification journey in the sustainability sector, and we're sure we will return to the topic in the coming months and years, when a number of the case studies and examples we have

CONCLUSION:
ARE YOU GAME?

described here have come to a level of maturity, and robust evaluations and analyses of their impacts have been calculated and mulled over. For the moment, and in particular for sustainability professionals in business and not-for-profit sectors, it is recommended a close eye is kept on what happens in this field over the next 12 months or so. As we hope to have demonstrated here, a simple gamification initiative can be easily implemented in a team or within an office environment, and could be a cost-effective way of testing the water in this new and potentially productive area.

Finally, we leave the closing words to Jane McGonigal, the ultimate games mistress in this emerging sector, who ends her book with the following thought:

"The great challenge for us today, and for the remainder of the century, is to integrate games more closely into our everyday lives, and to embrace them as a platform for collaborating on our most important planetary efforts."

....

Bibliography and Further Reading

Accenture. 2012. Scores, badges, leader boards and beyond: Gamification and sustainable behavior change, December. Available at: http://www.accenture.com/SiteCollectionDocuments/PDF/Accenture-Gamification-Sustainable-Behavior-Change.pdf

Bartle Richard: for information on the origin of player types: http://www.mud.co.uk/richard/hcds.htm

Chatfield, T. 2011. *Fun Inc: Why Games are the 21st Century's Most Serious Business* (London: Virgin Books).

Deloitte Tech Trends. 2012. Available at: http://www.deloitte.com/view/en_US/us/Services/consulting/technology-consulting/technology-2012/index.htm

Gartner Report on Gamification. April 2011. Available at: http://www.gartner.com/it/page.jsp?id=1629214

McGonigal, J. 2011. *Reality is Broken: How Games Can Change the World* (New York: Random House).

Pew Research Center. 2012. Gamification: Experts expect 'games layers' to expand in the future, with positive and negative results, 18 May. Available here: http://www.pewinternet.org/Reports/2012/Future-of-Gamification.aspx

Radoff, J. 2011. *Game On: Energize Your Business with Social Media Games* (New York: Wiley).

Shell, J. 2008. *The Art of Game Design: A Book of Lenses* (Boca Raton, FL: CRC Press).

Zicherman, G. and Cunningham, C. 2011. *Gamification by Design: Implementing Game Mechanics in Web and Mobile Apps* (Sebastopol, CA: O'Reilly).

Websites of interest and gamification case studies in the sustainability sector

Gamification sites of interest:

Business news Oracle on Bunchball board: http://www.gamification. co/2012/10/15/is-the-next-big-gamification-acquisition-imminent/

Gamification WiKi: http://gamification.org/wiki/Gamification

Donation website: DoNation.org.uk

One blogger's attempt to gamify his life: http://lifehacker.com/5975824/ gamify-your-life-a-guide-to-incentivizing-everything

Ecoinomy, company producing online-based employee engagement tools: http://www.ecoinomy.com/

Environmentally focused games and websites

Ecogamer, a website that collates a number of environmentally focused games: http://ecogamer.org/

E.On energy company game for children for reducing energy use: http:// games.211games.com/f/eon.swf

Earth Echo to the rescue: http://www.gamification.co/2012/10/16/

sgn-earth-echo-and-rescue-reef/

Games for Change, an organisation set up to advance social good through digital games environment: **Gamesforchange.com**

Gaming for Good, a PSFK initiative that challenged the world's top creative industries to come up with concepts that addressed issues put forth by the Climate Reality Project, this presentation displays the shortlisted games: **http://www.psfk.com/publishing/gaming-for-good**

Games 4 Sustainability, a website in development, but aims to draw a number of sustainability-focused games together on one site: **https://games4sustainability.com/**

Logicity, an online game for young people that aims to educate people on reducing their carbon footprint: **http://www.logicity.co.uk/**

London Science Museum, climate change related game Rizk: **http://www.sciencemuseum.org.uk/rizk**

'Paying to pollute', a simulated cap and trade carbon emissions game: **http://www.nbcnews.com/id/18288820/**

Red Redemption, Fate of the World game, a strategy game that simulates real social and environmental impacts of global climate change: **http://fateoftheworld.net/**

WWF/Allianz CEO2 game, player assumes role of CEO in one of four major industries (automotive, insurance, chemical or utility) in time period between 2010 and 2030. Aim of the game is to show how certain investments can lead to profitable growth in low-carbon economy: **http://knowledge.allianz.com/ceo2/en_ext.html**

....

References

1. Fitocracy – the online social game that makes the participation in physical games and exercise more fun by sharing goals and successes at **https://www. fitocracy.com/** and MyFitnessPal at **http://www.myfitnesspal.com**

2. The Foldit Project. A crowd-sourced, point-scoring medically related challenge thrown out to non-professionals to accurately define and replicate an AIDs-related protein enzyme.

3. **Saveup.com**. Reuters report at **http://www.reuters.com/article/2012/01/13/ us-usa-gamification-idUSTRE80C19M20120113** turns looking after your personal finances into a game.

4. Chore Wars, an online 'Alternate Reality Game' (ARG) that aims to convert banal, routine chores into activities that people enjoy doing by making them into a competition with points awarded for chores completed, at **www.chorewars.com**.

5. Bunchball history at **http://www.bunchball.com/about/milestones**.

6. Gamification wiki at **http://gamification.org/wiki/Gamification**.

7. Gartner Enterprise Architecture Summit, Egham, Surrey, 2011, at **http://www. gartner.com/it/page.jsp?id=1629214**.

8. Deloittes Tech Trends, Elevate IT for digital business, 2012 report.

9. Fitocracy and MyFitnessPal. See note 1.

10. The Foldit Project – see note 2.

11. **Saveup.com** – see note 3.

12. Chore Wars – see note 4.

REFERENCES

13. Pew Research Center (2012) Gamification: Experts expect 'games layers' to expand in the future, with positive and negative results, 18 May.

14. Gamification in 2012: Market update, consumer and enterprise market trends M2 research.

15. The Common Cause: The case for working with values and frames has a good range of readings on the topic of what motivates people to action at http://valuesandframes.org/.

16. View the video here: http://www.youtube.com/watch?v=0dOfBEm5DZU. Read the ASA's ruling on the complaints made against the series of adverts here: http://www.asa.org.uk/Rulings/Adjudications/2010/3/Department-of-Energy-and-Climate-Change/TF_ADJ_48225.aspx.

17. *No Pressure* is no longer available to view but a good synopsis of the plot can be read here: http://en.wikipedia.org/wiki/No_Pressure_(film).

18. News article from the Huffington Post: http://www.huffingtonpost.com/2011/09/19/aids-protein-decoded-gamers_n_970113.html. Foldit experiment's official website and blog: http://fold.it/portal/blog.

19. The game, the Royal Game of Ur can be found here: http://www.mesopotamia.co.uk/tombs/challenge/cha_set.html.

20. http://www2.fiat.co.uk/ecodrive/#ecodrive/intro.

21. The Act on CO_2 calculator can be found here: http://carboncalculator.direct.gov.uk/index.html.

22. The Act on CO_2 methodology paper, with an explanation of the 'Compare with Other Users' tool can be found on page 50 of the following publication: http://carboncalculator.direct.gov.uk/assets/METHODOLOGY%20PAPER%20FINAL.pdf.

23. The Donation website: http://thedonation.org.uk/.

24. DoNation Survey results, February 2012.

25. Wessex Water mobile app game 'Bag It and Bin It'.

26. www.linkedin.com.

27. www.cloudapps.co.uk.

28. www.ecoinomy.com.

29. www.greenrewards.co.uk.

30. The average combined gas and electricity bill in the UK in 2012 is approximately £1276; DECC energy price update, December 2012.

31. http://blog.opower.com/2012/08/gamification-and-energy-consumption/.

32. http://www.opower.com/company/news-press/press_releases/57?web SyncID=eb788ae5-eb23-1dbe-7ba9-48a1bdd7a410&sessionGUID=20a33 228-b27e-4e09-4a06-1b9327267ecd.

33. http://newshub.aetna.com/press-release/member-and-consumer-health/ aetna-and-mindbloom-gamify-wellness-help-drive-healthy-habi.

34. Info-Sys Stanford Traffic Project: http://simula.stanford.edu/Incentive_ mechanisms/Instant.html.

35. http://simula.stanford.edu/Incentive_mechanisms/Instant_results.html.

36. Accenture (2012) Scores, badges, leader boards and beyond: Gamification and sustainable behavior change, December, at: http://www.accenture. com/SiteCollectionDocuments/PDF/Accenture-Gamification-Sustainable-Behavior-Change.pdf.

. . . .

Lightning Source UK Ltd.
Milton Keynes UK
UKOW04n1310230715

255713UK00003B/40/P

9 781909 293946